God Doesn't
Believe In Atheists

Ray Comfort

Ray Comfort
Living Waters Publications
P.O. Box 1172
Bellflower CA 90706

ISBN 1-878859-01-3

NKJV used unless otherwise indicated

Cover design Steve Hunt

Printed in the United States of America

ACKNOWLEDGEMENTS
My sincere thanks to Patti Papazian; to Garry Ansdell and
Deb Petroski for their valuable editorial assistance and
Ken Van Mersbergen for his computer expertise.

DEDICATION

To my lovely wife Sue, our friends Jerry and Debbie Loveall, Steve and Cathy Gallatin, Dick Dillehay, Skip, Jeff and the folks at Living Epistles and my three offspring, Jacob, Rachel and Daniel.

CONTENTS

According to *T.V. Guide*, there are ten million atheists in the United States. The atheistic *Freedom From Religion Incorporated* maintains that there are *twenty* million. They may be lying, but who really cares about a ten million exaggeration if there's no higher power to answer to? Personally, I don't think there are *any* atheists in the United States. Let me tell you why. . .

Atheism - N. The belief that there is no God <MF Gk <*a* - without + *Theos* God>

CHAPTER 1
WHO MADE GOD?

Someone with a dry wit once made me laugh when he mumbled, "Come in boat number nine. Please come in boat number nine. . .boat number nine. . .can you hear me? Wait a minute. . .*we don't have a boat number nine!* Boat number six. . .are you in trouble?"

It amazes me that the world can have a belief in the existence of God (96 percent of Americans believe in God), and yet not think for a minute that something is radically wrong. They can smile while boat number six sits up-side-down on the water, slowly sinking.

Let's look at an average day on God's fair earth. The day dawns to find that, according to UNICEF, 20,000 children have starved to death during the night. Another 20,000 children and many thousands of adults will die today of severe malnutrition. Nothing new there. Literally hundreds of people will die from snake bites (an estimated 35,000 each year), poisonous spiders, sharks attacks (an average of 28 per year), scorpion bites, be eaten by lions, tigers, and devoured by other man-eating killers, not to mention blood sucking fleas, mosquitos and leeches.

Perhaps today we may have a surprise volcanic eruption, or an earthquake to crush families to death beneath the debris of their homes. Cancerous diseases will again take their toll and cause thousands to die in agony. Multitudes will perish from fatal ailments that plague and have always plagued mankind, from asthma to typhoid to leprosy to heart disease. Today, human beings will be struck by lightning, drown in floods, be stung to death by killer bees, killed by hurricanes and tornadoes, tormented by blights, pestilence and infestations; they will be afflicted, devastated and brought to ruin.

The fact is, either
>1/ There is no God, evidenced by the chaos,
>2/ God is totally incompetent and can't control His creation (or *won't*, which makes Him a tyrant), or
>3/ There is another explanation; one which the Bible gives for the state of the world.

First, let's take a rational, logical look at the first of these three thoughts; a philosophy commonly called "atheism."

FAITH IS FOR WIMPS

From my own personal experience and from listening to many objections to Christianity, I have found that the subject of "faith" is often offensive to the non-believer. My own pre-Christian philosophy was that faith was for the weak-minded, for little old ladies and for those near death. Yet every belief you and I have about history, about other countries, about science, about biology, etc., exists because of faith. You only believe what you believe because you believed the person who told you the information you believe. You don't *know* who discovered America; you have faith that what was told to you is indeed true. Neither do you know if General Custer died at the hands of Indians or if Napoleon really did exist. We can't live without faith. Try it. Say to yourself, "Today, I refuse to exercise any faith at all!" Then before you eat your corn flakes, go through every flake, scientifically testing it before you will eat it; refuse to trust that the manufacturers have obeyed health regulations and mixed ingredients correctly.

Do the same tests on the milk before you pour it on the corn flakes, in faith. You don't know that the milk manufacturers have done their job and given you pure milk. They may have mixed in something that could be harmful to your health. Don't you trust the sugar producers either. Who knows what they did while processing the sugar? Check up on the microscope and other tools used for your analysis; how can you really trust that the information being gathered from them is reliable? Don't trust your weight to the chair at the breakfast table. Don't believe today's weather report or any news item until you actually go to the location of the item and see for yourself if what they would have you believe is true. Then you will have to trust your natural senses.

Before you drink your coffee, don't just trust that the cup is clean; wash it out yourself. Don't use untested water in faith. Who knows what's in it nowadays! Analyze the coffee. If you decide to take a taxi to work, you will have to trust your life to a taxi and the taxi driver and the other drivers to stay on their side of the road. You will have to trust elevators, stairways, airplanes, the post office, and banks. Believe me. . .it's either live with faith or paranoia.

If then faith so surrounds us, why should it be so offensive? It is because faith is as essential to the spiritual as oxygen is to the natural. If a professing atheist can get rid of faith, he can get rid of Christianity. In trying to do so, he saws through the branch he is sitting on. *His own faith in the erroneous information he has makes him think that he is atheistic in his beliefs.*

TRUMP-CARD

From experience, I have found that the fashionable atheist's question, "Where did God come from?" does not deserve a question mark. It is usually presented as a statement of rhetoric. The "questioner" is of the persuasion that such a question cannot be answered. A twinkle is usually seen in the eye as he tosses what he believes is his trump card onto the table. He gambles his very soul on the fact that there is no higher card. . . *that it can't be answered.*

Actually, the explanation is very simple. Answer me this: Does space have an end? If it does. . .that is, there is a block wall at the end of space which says, "The End," *then I want to know what's behind the block wall!* By faith, you and I are forced to believe that whatever direction we set off into, space will never end. It just goes on and on, and on. . .forever. It has no beginning or ending. It hurts the brain to think about it, but we have no choice but to accept that fact by faith.

14

God also has no beginning and no end. But with God, we have a little more information. Time is a dimension God has created and subjected man to. You and I have to wait for time to pass. You can't go ahead even a minute in time. You are enslaved in its power; and because you are in time, logic, reason, and rationalism demand a "beginning" and an "end." *It hurts the brain to think of any other dimension.*

TIMELESSNESS
God is not subject to the dimension of time. He dwells in eternity. The Bible tells us that "a day to the Lord is a thousand years to us." You can prove this for yourself by studying the prophecies of the Bible dealt with in a chapter of this book. God can flick through time as you and I flick through pages of a history book. If you find this hard to believe, even with the evidence of biblical prophecies staring at you, you will find it to be true one day. The Scriptures tell us that God will eventually withdraw time. Then we will dwell in eternity.

The Christian is told that he understands "by faith." In other words, just as I trust a surgeon even though I have no real understanding of *how* he is going to operate, I understand that is how the whole thing operates. So in the same manner I trust God. Many have died at the hands of surgeons, but no one perishes in the hands of God. Faith in God is "sure and steadfast, an anchor to the soul." Doctors will fail you, pilots will fail you, friends you trust will disappoint you, elevators will let you down, but the promises of Almighty God are totally trustworthy. This may be hard for you to swallow at this point of time, but have an open mind as we look closely at the subject of atheism in the next few chapters.

CHAPTER 2
THE ATHEIST TEST

I don't believe in atheists. This isn't because I haven't met people who claim the title, but because there *cannot* be such a person. Let me explain why by asking you two questions.

First, do you know the combined weight of all the sand on all the beaches on the islands of Hawaii? *Do you?* I think I can assume that you don't, which brings us to the second question. Do you know how many hairs are on the back of an adult male Tibetan yak? Do you know? Probably not. So I think it is reasonable for me to conclude that there are some things you don't know.

Let's say that you do know three-quarters of all the knowledge in the universe. You know almost everything and everybody. There is hardly a rock in the universe that you are not intimately familiar with, or a grain of sand that you are not aware of. You know almost all that has happened in history, from that which is common knowledge to the minor details of the secret love life of Napoleon's grandmother's black cat's fleas. *You know an*

17

incredible three-quarters of all things.

In the quarter of knowledge you have not yet come across, might there be ample evidence to prove the existence of God? If you are reasonable, you will be forced to admit that it is possible. Somewhere, *in the knowledge you haven't yet come across,* there could be ample evidence to prove that God does exist.

Let's look at the same thought from another angle. If I was to make an absolute statement such as, "There has never been an armed tank in the grounds of the White House," what is it that I need for that statement to be true? I need absolute or total knowledge. I need to have been stationed in the grounds of the White House since it was constructed, always keeping a watchful eye upon it both day and night until this moment in time. Had I left that place, and an armed tank appeared on the grounds, *even for a moment,* I have no basis for the statement. I need absolute knowledge before I can make an absolute statement. Conversely, to say, "There *has* been an armed tank in the grounds of the White House," I don't need to have all knowledge. I just need to have seen one, and the statement is then true.

To say categorically, "There is no God," is to make an absolute statement. For the statement to be true, I must know *for certain* that there is no God in the entire universe. No human being has all knowledge; therefore none of us is able to truthfully make the assertion.

If you insist upon disbelief in God, what you must say is,

"Having the limited knowledge I have at present, I believe that there is no God." Owing to a lack of knowledge on your part, you don't know if God exists; so in the strict sense of the word, you *cannot* be an atheist. The only true qualifier for the title is the One who has absolute knowledge. . . and why on earth would God want to deny His own existence?

The professing atheist is, in truth, what is commonly known as an "agnostic." It is interesting to note that the Latin equivalent for the Greek word is "ignoramus," which seems appropriate for those who say they don't know if God exists when creation is staring at them in the face. What would you think of the mental capacity of someone who looked at a building and didn't know if there was a builder? The Bible tells us that this ignorance is "willful," i.e. a choosing to remain in rebellious ignorance. It's not that he *can't* find God, but that he *won't.* The atheist can't find God for the same reason a thief can't find a policeman. He knows that if he admits there is a God, he is admitting that he is ultimately responsible to Him. . .not a pleasant thought for some.

DELAYED ANSWER

Before my conversion, I could not deny the existence of God. This was because of two basic reasons. First, I had an inner knowledge deep within my heart that God required that He be first in my affections. Second, things that were made told me that there was a Maker, "For that which is known about God is evident to them and made plain in their inner consciences, because God Himself has shown it to them. For since the creation of the world His invisible nature and attributes, that is, His eternal power and divinity have been made intelligible and clearly discernible in and through the things that have been made -- His handiwork. So men are without excuse -- altogether without any defence or justification" (Romans 1: 19 & 20 Amplified Bible).

GOD, STRIKE ME DEAD!

It is said that Mussolini, the Italian dictator, once stood on a pinnacle and cried, "God. . .if you are there, *strike me dead!*" When God didn't bow to his dictates, he then concluded that there was no God. However, his prayer was answered. . .some time later.

CHAPTER 3
BANANA IN HAND

Is it possible to prove if God does exist? To answer this, let me share with you my theory of where the Coca Cola can may have come from:

Millions of years ago, an incredible explosion sent a massive rock spinning through space. As it cooled, a brown, sweet bubbly liquid formed on its surface. As time passed, tin crept out of the water and shaped itself into a can, (which coincidentally fits neatly into the human hand), formed itself a lid, then a tab on the lid. Approximately 500,000 years later, red and white paint fell from the sky and clung to the can, forming itself into the words, "COCA COLA Classic, Trade-mark, Original Formula 12 FL OZ (355 ML).

At this point of time, you may be feeling somewhat insulted, *and so you should*. Such irrationalism is beneath your intellectual dignity. You know that if the Coca Cola can has a design, there must be a designer; if it is made, there *must* be a maker. The alternative is unreasonable, illogical and unintelligent to say the least.

Now, to bring a point to what I am saying, I would appreciate it if you would be kind enough to go and find a banana. It will be well worth the effort.

EXHIBIT A

I presume you have the banana in hand. We will call it "Exhibit A." If you have found a well-made banana, you will notice that the far side has three ridges, and the close side has two ridges. Notice how neatly the banana fits into the human hand. Feel also how the fruit has been made with a non-slip surface. Note how the banana has been made with an outward indication of the inward condition of the contents -- green -- too early; yellow -- just right; black -- *too late*.

Take a look at the top of it and see how, like the Coca Cola can, it has been made with a "tab," so that it can be simply opened. Firmly pull the tab and see how there are perforations on the wrapper, so that it will peel into four pieces and hang gracefully over the hand. This wrapper is environmentally sound, being made of a completely bio-degradable substance, turning back into banana-growing soil in time.

Notice how the banana is the perfect size and shape for the human mouth, with a point at the top, for ease of entry. Put it into your mouth and give your taste buds a treat. Not only will your taste buds smile, but so will your whole body. The banana is full of body-building calories, and is easy for the stomach to digest. And what's more, the Maker of the banana has even curved it towards the face to make the whole eating process much easier.

EXHIBIT B

Now, if you would be kind enough, put the banana down and go get an apple. Take the apple in your hand and study its form. Notice how it's perfectly shaped for the human hand. All 10,000 different varieties are similarly shaped. The apple has an advantage over the banana in that you may eat the wrapper. On the inside, you will find a chewy mouth-watering substance, which is pleasant to the taste buds and beneficial for the body. When you get to the core of the substance, you will find something most of us take for granted. So that you won't be disheartened when the apple has gone, the Manufacturer has, completely free of charge, placed small black seeds in the middle. Amazingly, when these are placed into the soil, they form themselves into trees that produce more apples!

The professing atheist has ten million times more chance of convincing me that no one designed the Coca Cola can than he has of persuading me to believe that all created things have no Maker! Just as it's an insult to the intellect to say that paint "formed itself" into words on a can, it is infinitely more absurd to even momentarily entertain the thought that the whole of creation has no Creator.

What chance would I have of convincing you that this book had no author, printer or publisher? That everything came from nothing and formed itself into legible words on the paper; that the numbers on each page fell into order by mere chance? It then bound and trimmed itself into the paperback size. Could I even convince you that the design on the cover alone had no designer? Could you believe that the Mona Lisa had no artist? Did the paint "fall" onto the canvas? Do you know of any house that didn't have a builder?

CHAPTER 4
SEEING IS BELIEVING

The existence of God is what's known as an "axiom." An axiom is a self evident truth. The fact that parallel lines never meet is what's known as an axiom. If I were to devote my life to trying to either prove or disprove that parallel lines never meet, I lack in brainery. If the lines meet, they are not parallel, and if they are parallel, they will never meet. That is so obvious, it doesn't need to be proved or disproved; it is self-evident, an axiom.

The existence of God is an axiom. It is obvious that if there is a creation, there must be a Creator. For things to be "made," logic, reason, intellect and rationalism demand that there be a Maker. It should neither need to be proved or disproved.

Let's presume your problem is that you can't *see* God. Your philosophy is that "seeing is believing." If that is so, the next time you see water shimmering on a hot road, stop for a drink. Or the next time you watch a sunrise, and see the sun move across the sky, remind yourself that your eyes are lying to you. The sun neither rises, moves or sets; it remains still while the earth turns. The next time you

25

gaze at a blue sky, tell your eyes that they are not seeing right. The sky has no color -- ask any astronaut. Slight-of-hand magicians make their living based on the fact that seeing *isn't* believing.

We believe in plenty of things we can't see. For example, right behind you, beside you, and even right in front of you are masses of invisible television waves. Cowboys, Indians, news-readers, soap operas etc. are flashing before your eyes, but you can't see them; they are totally invisible. Think about this - *If I denied their existence because I couldn't see them, would that alter the reality of their existence?* Of course not.

BACK TO DA VINCI

Why do you believe a painting has a painter? Isn't it purely because of the existence of the painting? Do you insist on seeing Da Vinci before you believe that the Mona Lisa was painted? Do you insist on seeing the builder before you believe that the house you are in was built? Is that your criteria for belief? I doubt it. The house is ample proof that there was a builder.

Does the jumbo jet have no maker until you lay your eyes on those who made the aircraft? Think for a moment of the intricacies of the mechanics of the plane, of the technologically brilliant minds of the men who make them. Yet the human eye leaves the most complex creations of men, including the jumbo jet, in the dust of primitive technology. The most brilliant minds on the earth cannot begin to recreate an eye. If you lose one, the best modern science can do for you is give you a glorified marble to slip in the slot. We are still in the dark about its incredible workings. Do you realize that each eye you are using at the moment has 40,000,000 nerve endings on its inside. If you have the brain-power to make one nerve-ending, tell modern science so they can begin to see their way to making their first eye.

The fact is, we can't make anything from nothing. Find the most brilliant scientist in this world, put him in a laboratory and ask him to make something from nothing. *He can't do it.* He doesn't know how. We can *re-create, but we cannot create.* We can't even make one grain of sand from nothing! If that then is the case, how dare we even begin to think for a moment that all creation, the human body, animals, flowers, birds, trees, fruits, the seasons, the sun, the moon, the stars, etc. fell together by mere random chance!

ALBERT KNEW

Meditate for a moment on how the seasons of summer, fall, winter and spring come around each year in the same order. Scientists can predict the sunrise one hundred years from now with incredible accuracy -- to the second. Think of the earth, spinning as it orbits the sun, while our moon orbits the earth. Think of the moon pulling the tides of the sea in and out all over the earth, the plants breathing carbon dioxide, then giving out oxygen for us to breathe in, and then us giving out carbon dioxide for them to breathe in. Meditate on the sun evaporating seawater, clouds forming, being blown by the wind, rising in height over the mountains, dropping the rain to give life to the earth, and at the same time clearing the air of its impurities. Think of how the mountains hold much of the water in the form of snow, until the heat of summer melts it so that it will feed the rivers to water the land and pour into the sea; and so the incredible, and predictable life-cycle continues.

If you can't believe in things because you have never seen them, how then do you know you've got a brain. You've never seen it, and if you can look at this miraculous creation and say there's no Creator, then there's no evidence to say that it does exist. Nowhere does the Bible set out to prove that God exists; it just frankly states the obvious: "The fool has said in his heart, `There is no God.'"

I hope that such talk doesn't offend you. That's not my purpose. I want to show you that atheism is totally the opposite of what it professes to be -- unthinking. What is your I.Q.? Is it 120. . .140? Or have you higher intelligence? Are you round the 180 mark? Do you qualify for work at NASA? Or maybe you approach the intelligence of Einstein. Listen to one of the greatest minds ever made: "Everyone who is seriously interested in the pursuit of science becomes convinced that a spirit is manifest in the laws of the universe -- *a spirit vastly superior to man, and one in the face of which our modest powers must feel humble."* - Albert Einstein.

Perhaps the name "God" offends you. Well, let's put it aside for a moment and call it a force, higher power, or like Albert, a Spirit. Isn't it true that whatever or whoever made this universe must be awesome to say the least? What sort of supreme creative force could make something as incredible as the sun? Scientists tell us that this massive earth fits into the volume of the sun *one million times*! *Flames on the sun leap up three hundred and fifty thousand miles at a time.* But more than that, it is only a small sun of millions in the universe. It has been placed 93,000,000 miles from us so that it's just warm enough to maintain life. If it were a little closer, we would all die either from the heat or from drowning. In fact, if the polar ice melted and flooded the earth, the sea level would rise to a point where it would submerge the Empire State building up to the twentieth floor.

If the sun was further away however, we would all die by freezing. It is said that one second of energy given off by the sun is approximately 13,000,000 times greater than the average amount of electricity used each year in the whole United States. What sort of creative force could make that sun, then hold it in space and sustain its brilliance? Meditate on the thought for a moment.

How could this power make the human heart, form the ribs within the body of an unborn baby, make a human eye, or create the flesh which covers our body? How could it create the human mind with its unending complex corridors, its deepest thoughts and desires? It makes you think, doesn't it?

CHAPTER 5
STRAWBERRIES AND GARLIC

Do you realize that you sneeze at 120 miles per hour? Did you also know that every time you sneeze, you have been programmed to close your eyes? Where does your hair grow from? How can the thin layer of skin on your head send out a special type of hair? It has been formulated in your genes to send out a certain type of hair for the head; hair different from that which grows on the arms, or on the eyelids or the eyebrows. Imagine if you had eyebrows or eyelashes that grew to the length of the type of hair on your head. Think of the fine row of hair that makes up the eyelash, or of the way the hairs face the same direction on the eyebrow.

Have you ever studied the ordinary garden snail and wondered how its shell is able to grow in proportion to its body? When it's a baby snail, it has a baby shell. As it doubles in size, it doesn't discard it; the hard shell also doubles in size. Do you credit the snail with having a mind brilliant enough to make its own shell? How does a caterpillar get rid of all its legs while inside a cocoon, grow two fresh ones, then form itself into a butterfly?

Do you give a baby credit for having the ability to grow its own teeth? How did you grow both sets of yours? If you ever decide to get false teeth, will you have them made, or will you wait for "chance" to make a pair for you? Look at your fingernails. Where did they grow from? What makes up their substance? How is it that your lungs keep breathing, irrespective of your will? How does your subconscious mind continually feed you with thoughts, even when you sleep? Listen to it talk to you and keep you company. It never stops. Try and stop it yourself. Put this book down and try and think of nothing for five minutes. Bet you can't. Your subconscious mind has been set in motion, and it has little to do with your will.

Right at this moment, your liver, kidneys, heart, pancreas, salivary glands, etc. are all working to keep your body going. You don't even have the power to switch them off and on. During your sleep tonight, your heart will pump 75 gallons of blood through your body each hour.

THE GREATEST REFLECTION
Perhaps the greatest proof of the Creator's existence is seen when you gaze into the mirror. Contrary to common belief, your lungs are more than just bags to breathe smoke into. They are designed to filter oxygen out of the air you breathe. These organs contain 300,000,000,000 tiny blood vessels called capillaries. Your entire blood supply washes through your lungs once every minute. In your lifetime, the marrow in your bones will create approximately half a ton of red blood corpuscles.

You have focusing muscles in your eyes that move an

estimated 100,000 times each day. That same eye has within it a retina that covers less than a square inch and contains 137,000,000 light sensitive cells. A wide-eyed Charles Darwin said, "To suppose that the eye could have been formed by natural selection, seems, I freely confess, absurd in the highest degree." Your brain contains 10,000,000,000 neurons or microscopic nerve cells. Your stomach, which produces four pints of gastric juice each day, has 35,000,000 glands lining it. Next time you eat a delicious meal, be thankful for the 8,000 taste buds that were put into your mouth. Imagine how boring eating would be without them.

George Gallop, the famous statistician said, "I could prove God statistically; take the human body alone; the chance that all the functions of the individual would just happen, is a statistical monstrosity."

Was it an accident that your ears were designed to capture sound? The grooves, bumps and ridges are made to catch passing sound waves and channel them into the eardrum. Your hands were made to grip and feel: the tongue was made to taste food and to shape speech; the nose was made to smell. Imagine if you had been made in an impractical manner. What if your ears faced backwards, or your nose was upside down and could cause you to drown in the rain, or your mouth had two tongues? I am serious. If humanity just *happened*, with no purposeful design, why don't we see such creatures? In fact, we see the very opposite in creation. From the teeth of a dog to the legs of a grass-hopper, one can see practical design in every single thing that has been made.

Now, if the incredibly brilliant creative force made all things, then it is not only infinitely more intelligent than man whom it made, but it is surely familiar with what it has made. Not only did it create every one of the 100,000 hairs on the average non-bald human head, but it is also familiar with each individual hair. If the force can make the eye, it is not blind itself.

Creation reflects the genius of the Creator's hand. Let's look at a common cow. How is it that a brown cow eats green grass, which turns into white milk, then yellow butter, which is eaten by a man who grows red hair and has blue eyes? Imagine if you were able to invent a machine that could turn your grass cuttings into milk; yet the cow does just that. Tell me how she does it. If it is so simple, make your millions by inventing the grass-cuttings-into-milk-machine. Is the cow wiser than you? Explain to me how a sparrow knows he is a sparrow and stays with other sparrows, or how a baby knows how to look into the eyes of its mother when no one has taught it. Explain how a tree growing on a steep hillside grows upward and not at right angles to the cliff. Tell me how strawberries can grow right next to garlic, and yet both derive their own unique taste from the same soil and water. How was a wasp made so that its wings flap at 100 beats every second, or the housefly at 190 per second, or the mosquito at an amazing 500 beats every second?

The most godless must be humbled by a sense of awe and wonder when standing beneath the mighty power of Niagara Falls, or as he gazes into the Grand Canyon, or stares into the infinity of space. How much more should we be humbled by the *Maker* of these things?

CHAPTER 6
GIVE ME WATER

I once saw a T.V. news reporter say, "Tonight we will look at the buying and selling of the world's most priceless commodity. . . *information*." He was right, information *is* the world's most priceless commodity. If you have information as to where oil deposits are, or you have information about the location of gold or diamonds in the earth, you can be a billionaire overnight. *Information can even save your life*. If you are in a building that is on fire and you know the location of the fire escapes, you can find your way out. If you are without that information, you will probably die. Your actions will be governed by information, or more precisely, what you *do* with that information will govern your actions.

A man in the U.S. once wanted to paint his steep A frame roof. As his ladder was too short to reach the top, he threw a strong rope over the roof, went around the other side, and carefully secured the rope to the back of his car. Then he went around the back of the house, climbed up onto his roof, tied the rope firmly around his waist, and began painting. His wife, not knowing what he had done, came out of the house, car keys in hand, got into the car *and drove off*. He was pulled over the top of the roof and was seriously injured.

Perhaps you see nothing wrong with believing the theory of evolution, even if it can't be substantiated. But remember, *your information will govern your actions.* If you believe a drink contains poison, you won't drink it. If you believe it is O.K., you will drink it. If you believe evolution is true, and from that premise believe that the Bible is false, you won't then repent. Like the man who secured himself to the car, you will find you are only as secure as to that to which you secured yourself. If your faith is in evolution and not God's promises, you will find that what you have tied yourself to, will be your eternal downfall. You will perish because you refused information that would have saved your most prized possession.

DIAMONDS OR WATER?
Let me put it another way. If I offered you a fistful of diamonds or a bucket of cold water, which would you take? The diamonds of course. But if you were crawling through a desert, lips blistered, tongue swollen, dying of thirst, and I offered you a fistful of diamonds or a bucket of cool water, you would despise the diamonds and cry, *"Give me water. . .lest I die!"* That is called "circumstantial priorities." Your priorities change according to your circumstances.

Christianity demands a choice between the sparkling diamonds of sin and the cool, clear waters of everlasting life. Of course, you *far* prefer the diamonds of sin, something quite normal for sin-loving humanity. But on Judgment Day your circumstances will radically change. You will find yourself in the desert of God's judgment, upon your face, about to perish under the burning heat of a Creator who warns us that He's a "consuming fire." You despised the Water of Life when it was offered to you in Christ. Now you must face eternal consequences. Those sparkling diamonds you so dearly hold will suddenly be the glaring evidence for your condemnation.

Years ago, a television advertisement had a deep-voiced commentator ask the sobering question, "What goes through the mind of a driver at the moment of impact in a head-on collision if he's not wearing a seat belt?" As he spoke, they showed a dummy without a safety belt, in slow motion, reacting to a head-on collision. As the dummy moved forward on impact, the steering wheel went right through its skull. Then the commentator somberly continued, ". . . *the steering-wheel*. . .you can learn a lot from a dummy. *Buckle up!!"*

How could the censors allow such obvious fear tactics? This advertisement struck trepidation in the hearts of motorists. The reason is very clear. They were speaking the truth. It *is* a fearful thing to be in a head-on collision and not be wearing a seat-belt!

What I'm telling you is the Gospel truth. The Bible warns, *"It is a fearful thing to fall into the hands of the Living God!"* It is right that you should fear because you are in danger of eternal damnation without the Savior. You are going to collide head on with God's Law. Let Judgment Day play before your eyes in slow motion. Look closely at the fearful consequences of not buckling yourself into the salvation of God.

COZY COCOON

I will never forget a very interesting B.B.C. documentary. I watched in amazement as they gave air-time to a man *playing castanets to his tomatoes*.

Then the program moved from the sublime to the insane. This gentleman placed earphones onto his tomatoes and played classical music to them -- in stereo, of course. Obviously a "nut" entertaining fruit!

I was about to turn the T.V. off in disgust when I heard something that radically changed my mind. This man's name was in *The Guiness Book of Records* for having the world's largest tomato -- *four and a half pounds!* I learned a valuable lesson that day -- don't knock something until you see its results.

Next time you see a caterpillar on a leaf, study him for a while. You will notice that he twists and turns until he has wound himself into a web, finally encasing himself into a cocoon. We don't knock what he's doing because we know that metamorphosis is taking place within the cocoon. A miracle of nature is happening. In time, a beautiful butterfly will appear.

To those who don't understand, Christians are doing no more than wrapping themselves into the bondage of rules and regulations, hiding from the real world in the cocoon of Christianity. But wait. . . *don't knock it until you see the results!* When you look at the Church of today, you're looking at the grub. Granted, we do seem to lack in so many areas. But the same One who created metamorphosis is all the while at work in the hearts of those that love Him, and the day will come when the butterfly will emerge.

LIGHT RELIEF

This may seem unthinkable, but imagine if the Bible, Jesus Christ, Almighty God, the Creator of the universe is right, and you are wrong! Imagine that. . .*you wrong?* Look at it this way. If you are right, and there is no Creator, no after-life, no justice, no Heaven and no Hell, you won't even get the chance to say, *"I told you so!"* If you are right, then creation was an accident, the Bible is but fables, Jesus Christ was a liar, and what's more, *I have spent hours pouring my heart out in this book for nothing!* But if what I am saying is true, the atheist will get the shock of his death. He will wake up dead! He will find that he truly has "passed on." I ask again, is it possible that you could be wrong? Come on, bend a little. . .(just between you and me). Have you ever been wrong? Are you divinely infallible? Are you different from the rest of us? Human nature is prone to error; the person who invented the eraser on the pencil knew that. To make the point (and for a little light relief), I submit the following evidence of human error. I don't do this in condescension, because I know that none of us is inflammable (. . .I mean infallible), we all make mistakes.

These are actual sentences taken from letters received by a large city's welfare department in applications for support:

1. I am forwarding my marriage certificate and six

children. I have seven, but one died which was baptized on a half sheet of paper.

2. I am writing the Welfare Department to say that my baby was born two years old. When do I get my money?

3. You have changed my little boy to a girl. Will this make a difference?

4. I cannot get sick pay. I have six children. Can you tell me why?

5. I am glad to report that my husband who is missing is dead.

6. This is my eighth child. What are you going to do about it?

7. Please find for certain if my husband is dead. The man I am now living with can't eat or do anything till he knows.

8. I am very much annoyed to find you have branded my son illiterate. This is a dirty lie as I was married a week before he was born.

9. In answer to your letter, I have given birth to a boy weighing ten pounds. I hope this is satisfactory.

10. I am forwarding my marriage certificate and three children, one of which is a mistake as you can see.

11. Unless I get my husband's money pretty soon, I will be forced to live an immortal life.

12. In accordance with your instructions I have given birth to twins in the enclosed envelope.

CHAPTER 7
STRONGER THAN THE SEX-DRIVE

Years ago I knew a man in his twenties, who was told by his doctor that he had six months to live. His non-Christian friends advised him, "Do a brothel crawl, and enjoy the last six months of your life!" He wasn't interested. He found deep within his heart, he had something *far* stronger than the sex-drive; it was his will to live. A cry came from his innermost being, "*Oh. . .I don't want to die!*" I'm sure every one of us can identify with that. No one in his right mind wants to die. That cry is God-given. The Bible tells us that God has put eternity in our hearts.

I once dropped a friend off at the local crematorium (he was alive at the time). As I sat in my car, I couldn't help noticing how pleasant they had the place looking. It had a nice clean block wall surrounding it, with a rose garden in front of it. The establishment was no longer called a mortuary, but was fondly known by most locals as the

Crem. Inside, the decor was extremely tasteful. The directors (no longer called "undertakers") didn't wear black, but a restrained green. Words were carefully chosen as not to offend. The graveyard was called a cemetery. The person isn't dead, he has deceased. The coffin, now called a casket, is surrounded by a frill, similar to that on a birthday cake. When your deathday comes, you get your own shiny casket, your own little plot of ground, with a personal name-plate and your own little rose. . .kinda makes you look forward to your turn doesn't it? *No, No - - a thousand times no!* It doesn't matter how much death is dressed up, no one (in his right mind) wants to try it on for size!

ROCK AROUND THE CLOCK
Recently I struck up a conversation with a tall, good-looking surfer from Australia. After getting to know him, I swung the discussion around to Christian things. He was very open; in fact, he shared something with me that he hadn't told another soul. He'd been out on his surfboard when a friend had casually said, "See that big rock over there? That'll be here a thousand years after we're dead and gone." This young man had been so shaken by the gravity of the thought that he paddled in and sat soberly on the beach for twenty minutes. How could a dumb, unthinking, inanimate object such as a rock still be around *thousands of years after he died!*

Such solemn thoughts are the beginnings of an awakened mind. My first thoughts in that direction came to me when I was about seven years old. My brother took me to see a movie about the French revolution. Rich people were taken from prison by blood-thirsty, murderous peasants and paraded through the streets of Paris, tied hand and foot. Then they were cruelly mocked, pushed to the guillotine and their heads were chopped off. Just the thing for an impressionable seven-year-old.

Around the chopper sat the most ugly old hags you've ever seen. Each time a head rolled, they would scream with sheer delight, grin a toothless grin, then knit another stitch on their scarves to celebrate and keep count. The scarves were ten or fifteen feet in length.

It made me think, "*How horrible*. . .to be waiting in prison to die;" yet as time progressed, I saw that I too was on death row. With all of humanity, I awaited execution. Our holding cell is rather large, with a blue roof, good ventilation and bright lighting. We can move around this vast earth if we wish, but we are all still waiting for the chopper to come down. Andy Williams struck a note of truth when he sang, "Ain't it true, no matter what you do, they're gonna bury you, beneath the cold, cold ground. Big or tall, or long or short or fat or small. . .it's gonna get you all." The Bible gives the reason for this. God, the Judge of the Universe, has proclaimed the death sentence upon all humanity: "The soul that sins, it shall die." Proof of our sin, will be our death.

PLAYING CHICKEN
I heard of a portion of road on which there were continual fatalities. Drivers, despite warning signs, would speed around this corner and be killed. Finally, one of the local councilmen had a bright idea. He suggested putting

chickens on the side of the road. They did, and fatalities dramatically dropped; the drivers slowed down for the sake of the chickens! It would seem that the speedsters saw the danger of speed for chickens, but not for themselves. Why? Because inherent within each of us is this senseless idea that "It will never happen to me." It's always the "other guy" who gets killed. It's always the other guy who gets cancer. I guarantee that every single person who died before us had the *I never thought it would ever happen to me!* attitude.

A friend once refused to put on a car seat belt, saying, "I'm not planning to have an accident." I told him that takes the cake for the world's dumbest statement. There has *never* been a "planned" accident. If it is an accident, it is not planned; and if it's planned, it's not an accident. The dictionary says an accident is "Any thing occurring unexpectedly."

Sadly, that's the way death comes to most.

I was heckled while open-air preaching for many years by a man called Willie. He would say, almost daily, "When I see God, I'm going to spit in His face! Then I'm going to say, "What about this !!"*'.!!* Ray Comfort!" Well Willie is dead. He died of a heart attack one day. I know that he also had the attitude that it would never happen to him. Much to his shock and ours, it happened to him.

Someone once said, "There are only two things in life that are sure -- death and taxes." That's just not true. Plenty of people avoid taxes. . .nobody avoids death. We are all part of the ultimate statistic, ten out of ten die. The leading actor of a popular T.V. series, put it this way, "Death is a guarantee from the day we are born. But I guess we don't think about it because we think it will never happen." How right he was.

CHAPTER 8
WORMS TRANSFORMED

Imagine your amazement if you turned on the television to see a news item that reported:

"Scientists have just invented a machine which is able to turn your kitchen waste into a small white edible packet of food, which is surrounded by a hygienically-sealed protective casing. When this packet is opened, the contents may be eaten in a variety of delicious ways.

"It doesn't matter what type of food waste is put into the machine the night before, it always comes out the same consistent yellow and white color the next morning. In fact, even if fat, spinach, bread-crusts, apple-cores, wheat, and even live grubs and worms are put into it, *all are miraculously transformed overnight into a delicious-tasting food by the next morning.*

"Excited scientists report that, at a particular point in time, this incredible machine may be placed with a similar model, which will give it the ability to reproduce of itself. Yes, believe it or not, it can then make a special hygienically sealed packet which produces, you guessed it, another food-making machine! At any time, any of these machines themselves can be easily dismantled, cooked and eaten. They are said to taste finger lickin' good.'"

I'm sure that most of us would view such a news item with great skepticism, yet that is what we have with the ordinary, common, everyday chicken. Each day, most of the 4,000,000,000 chicken brains do what modern man's brain can't: they make eggs and chickens. Is the chicken more intelligent than man? Probably not. Therefore, something superior to man must have made the chicken. "Accident," is the alternative.

Aristotle said, "God, having become unseen to every nature, through His works is seen." Plato said, "The world must have a cause, and that cause is the Eternal Maker." Cicero echoed, "What can be so clear when we look at the sky and the heavenly bodies is that there is some deity of surpassing mind by whom these are governed?"

MADE FOR EACH OTHER
Without getting into blushing territory, think how, in almost all of creation, the male and the female are made for each other. From spiders to elephants, to man, to birds and bees, each is designed for reproduction. Like nut and bolt, they are made to perfectly come together. For the male spider to be made without a maker, that is, "chance" threw together its arms, legs, heart, liver, lungs, skin, brain, muscles, eyes and ears, not to mention its reproductive organs, is utterly unthinkable. But to add to the thought that it just so happened that accident also threw together the *female* spider, with its arms, legs, brain, muscles, eyes, etc., and just happened to throw in necessary reproductive

parts, *is nothing short of insane.* It is intellectual suicide. Yet the professing atheist has that belief.

Add to these thoughts the fact that there are *literally thousands* of different species of spider, all with spider organs, all having both male and female. If they didn't have both sexes, the species wouldn't be with us today. They would have died when the first male died, as there would only be one of each species. Think of all the different types of animals: the lion, tiger, bear, horse, cow, dog, cat, camel, giraffe, zebra, etc. Notice how each of them have two eyes, two specially designed ears, a brain, one mouth, one tongue, specially designed teeth, taste buds, one heart, kidneys, a pancreas, etc. as well as male and female, each having appropriate reproductive parts. Think of all the different birds: the sparrow, the chicken, the kiwi, the eagle, the hawk, the peacock, etc. Notice how they too have been given two eyes, two ears, one brain, etc. and each has male and female. Fish follow the same pattern. The male and female have been made with purpose in mind. This incredible, consistent order in created life shows a supremely intelligent and ordered mind in the Maker. If you deny that fact, go make a bird. I don't mean a wooden one; I mean a living, breathing, seeing, hearing, thinking, flying one. And by the way, make it from nothing.

LOOK, A COINCIDENCE!

Imagine I was carrying a large bag of oranges to my car. You walked away for a few minutes, then returned to hear me say, *"Hey, look on the ground! The bag ripped and all the oranges fell out!"* You look on the ground and see forty-five oranges in nine perfect rows, each of five oranges. What chance would those oranges have, all forty-five of them, of "falling" into nine perfectly straight rows of five? For *five* oranges to fall out of a bag and land in a line would be amazing, but for forty-five to do that, is too much for an intelligent mind to believe. Someone with an ordered mind placed them there. . .their order tells you that.

Imagine I had a new car, but I peeled off the maker's nameplate. Would you then think that the car had no maker because you could neither see the maker nor his name? No, you would know that an intelligent brain designed the vehicle because it had been made with purpose in mind. Take for instance the windshield. It is clearly more than ornamental. It is a functional part of the car, in that it has been made so that those in the car can see where they are going. It has been especially fitted with windshield wipers so that the windshield may be kept clear. The manufacturer has even fitted the car with little squirters so that it may be moistened for clarity of vision. *The car has been made with purpose in mind.*

Your Maker has given you two windshields to see out of. The wipers He has fitted are infinitely more sophisticated than that of any made by a modern car manufacturer. They clean your windshields simultaneously at the incredible speed of *one five hundredth of a second*. The process, which takes place irrespective of your will, happens so quickly that you don't even see it happen. If you are an average person, you have cleaned your windshield approximately 60 times since beginning this chapter. You've even been given little squirters called "tear ducts," which squirt clear water onto your windshields from the corners of both your eyes, keeping them lubricated so that the wipers can be more effective. Without the tear ducts, the eyes would probably dry up. Try drinking milk each day and see if the lubricant comes out white. Somehow you filter out the coloring of the liquids you drink, so that the cleaning liquid is clear, and doesn't cloud your vision.

HEAVY THOUGHTS

Speaking of clouded vision, I was once looking at clouds from the underside and had a strange thought. I began meditating on the fact that when I clean my car, I often carry a bucket of water to it. The bucket, when filled with water is very heavy. If water is heavy and clouds are full of water, clouds must be very heavy.

The next step was to call weather experts and see whether I was correct in my assumption. I explained my thoughts, then asked the question, "Are clouds heavy?" "Yes sir," came the firm reply. In fact (at the risk of making you fearful to step outside), the average summer rain-cloud weighs *hundreds of thousands of tons!* When I asked what holds the clouds in the sky, the expert explained that clouds are made of water vapor, which forms itself into drops. When the water becomes drops, the drops drip. Or to put it more clearly, when the drips form into drops, the drips drop.

The weather expert was full of enthusiasm as he answered my questions. At last, someone was drawing on his expertise. But the moment I mentioned any thought of the cloud-Maker, he didn't want to talk any longer. Strange.

CHAPTER 9
TOMBSTONE FACE

I don't know if you have noticed, but almost every time there is a mass disaster, a ship sinks or multitudes are killed by an earthquake, the traditional church is called upon to bury the dead. I feel saddened that so much of the world equates what they stand for with biblical Christianity. A few moments studying the Scriptures should show that there is a difference. Yet literally hundreds of millions are deceived into thinking that they are one in the same.

Religion is man's self-righteous efforts to reach God; in Christ, God reached down to man. History has shown that the greatest enemy to Christianity is what is commonly called organized religion. Jesus was murdered by men who professed to love God. Throughout the Book of Acts, the established religious leaders opposed the early Christians. No doubt such will be the case at the end of this age.

My distaste for established religion is lacking in conviction compared to the damnation proclaimed by the apostle

Paul on those who profess to be godly, and yet preach "another gospel," (see Galatians Chapter 1.)

At disaster time, the world calls upon the established church. The Bible is opened with nauseating predictability at Psalm 23. The page is then dusted, and read in monotone voice with tombstone face, ". . .though I walk through the valley of the shadow. . .of death. . .yet will I fear no evil. . ." It seems that they think that Psalm has something to do with death, when in fact it says the very opposite.

If I stand in the shadow of a wall, I'm not *in* the wall, I'm merely in close proximity to it. If I'm in the shadow of death, I'm not in death, I'm merely in close proximity to it. That's what the Bible says. *This life is the shadow of death.* Death casts its cold, dark shadow over us every minute of our breathing life. The Scriptures, speaking of the coming of the Messiah, said, "To them that sat in the shadow of death, a light has sprung up." When you come to Jesus Christ, the light of the world, you no longer "walk in darkness," but have the "Light of life." When someone receives Him who is the way, the truth, and "the life" through the power of the Holy Spirit, they don't receive a religion, they receive the very source of life itself. Just as light banishes darkness, so that life banishes death.

WHAT BLOTS OUT YOUR ETERNITY?
What is at the root of your convictions? For your own sake, ask yourself what hinders you coming to the Savior? Is it your pride? Do you prefer the praises of men to the praise of God? Do you fear man more than you fear

God? Perhaps you are afraid your friends will laugh at you. They won't. Your acquaintances will, but your *friends* won't; they'll respect you despite your beliefs. Perhaps it's your love of money. Will you, like the rich man fleeing from a sinking ship, put your gold into your pockets and drown because of its weight? Will you perish because of your riches? Remember when Jim Henson died unexpectantly? He had just sold his Muppet empire to the Disney Corporation for an estimated $100,000,000. How much did he take with him? There are no pockets in a shroud.

Recently Southern California police carried out an interesting "sting" operation. They had a list of literally thousands of wanted criminals who had somehow evaded jail. Instead of risking their lives by going and attempting to arrest them, they sent each a letter saying that the criminals had won a large amount of money in a free lottery.

The police put signs and banners on a building, placed balloons and even a clown on the outside to create a festive atmosphere, and to welcome the "winners." As each criminal entered the building, he heard music and celebration. He was then ushered into a room where he smiled as his hand was shaken. The facial expression changed from one of joy to unbelief as the person shaking his hand said, "Congratulations, you have just won a time in prison. . ." Literally dozens of criminals made their way through the main doors, were arrested and ushered out the back door. It was interesting to note that numbers of the lawbreakers said as they were apprehended, "I *thought* it was a sting operation!" but they couldn't stay away because of their greed. They were blinded to reason by their own love of money. Don't do the same. Think deeply about the issue of eternity. Say the word over and over to yourself.

WANTED: EYES

A long time ago, I purchased two Java sparrows for a bird aviary I had at the time. They were attractive birds, with smooth grey feathers and brightly colored beaks. As usual, the bird shop had placed them in a brown paper bag and stapled the top. It was a work day and some time before I went home, so I cut a small hole in the side of the bag and placed it on my office desk.

As the day passed, I was amazed at the pattern of human reaction. Most who stepped into my office wondered why on earth I had a moving paper bag on my desk. When I told them it was a bag of birds, they would pick it up, put their eye to the hole and say, "Wow! What sort of birds are they?" I took great delight in calmly saying, *"Mexican eye-peckers."* It's amazing how quickly a bag-hole can be pulled from the human eye. If we are so quick to care for the eye, how much more should we care for the soul, the very life that looks through the eye.

Imagine if you picked up a newspaper and saw the following advertisement: WANTED EYES: MUST BE FRESH. TRANSPLANT DOCTOR OFFERING $50,000 ONE EYE; $1,000,000 FOR MATCHING PAIR. All you have to do is go in and they will painlessly pluck them out. A million dollars - *now you can see the world!* No you can't. Sell your eyes and you sit in darkness until your death. How much would you sell your eyes for? Bet you wouldn't think of it. They are priceless. Yet they are just windows for the soul. If the eyes are priceless, how much must your soul be worth? The Bible says that it is without price. And if the soul is priceless, how much do you think God should sell *eternal life* for?

GOOD PEOPLE

When I became a Christian, I found myself in a dilemma. The Bible told me, "There is none good, no not one." Yet I knew many good people. The problem was that God's definition of good and mine were different. We may say a man is "good," because he's stopped stealing and reformed his ways. We think that good is merely "not bad." God's definition of good is perfection. . .*in thought, word and deed.*

Millions of religious people, and secular people for that matter, are being good, thinking that will merit entrance into Heaven. In essence, they are trying to purchase everlasting life by offering their good deeds to God in exchange for it. On judgment day, it will not be seen as a mere offer for purchase, but a detestable attempt to bribe God to forget our crimes against His Law.

Do you know of anyone who's "good"? Was Mother Teresa good? No, she needed Jesus Christ as her Savior; she admitted her sins. How about Mahatma Ghandi? Was he good? No, he said, "It is a constant torture to me that I am still so far removed from Him whom I know to be my very life and being. I know it is my own wretchedness and wickedness that keeps me from Him." He acknowledged his sins. Perhaps the only good person you can find is yourself. In truth, what we are really doing when we say that there are plenty of good people is attempting to justify our own sins. Let me speak to the wife of any man who says he's perfect. She will tell me the truth.

CHAPTER 10
I'LL RESURRECT HER FOR YOU

For the twelve years I spoke in "Speaker's Corner," it became a popular area for public speaking. On a bad day, I would always have at least twenty or thirty listeners. On a good day, it was normal to have two hundred listeners, 90 percent of whom were non-Christians. In 1986, however, I found myself on a soapbox on a sidewalk in Hawaii, speaking to a moving congregation; no one would stop! Sue and I had been flown thousands of miles to speak to about ninety young people from around the world. All week I spoke on evangelism, and now we were doing the practical. I expounded principles of fishing, now we were out to sea, but not a bite in sight. Things were getting desperate. It was then that I remembered a funeral drama I had written.

Having conducted a number of genuine funerals, I noticed that eyes and ears are wide open when ones are listening over the top of a dead loved one. So after a little organizing, I dressed as a priest and led six black-clad pall-bearers carrying a sheet-covered "corpse" down a main street of Honolulu.

As we marched, we were overtaken by a fire-engine towing a lifeboat. Suddenly, one of our group approached me and with wide eyes said, "Someone has drowned at Waikiki -- *right where we are going to do the drama!"* To do it there would have been in bad taste, so I went ahead to tell the "mourners" of the relocation. Unbeknown to me, an ex-military serviceman was standing on a street corner praying, "God. . .*where are You?"* when a priest walked by. He rushed after me, grabbed me by the arm, and began confessing his heart out to me. He was genuinely repentant, so I led him to the Lord.

I couldn't find the mourners. They had gone to look for us, so the new convert and I made our way back to where I had left the corpse and the pall-bearers. When we arrived, I could hardly get to them because of the crowd. Literally hundreds packed tightly around; *they thought we had the corpse that had drowned at Waikiki!* It turned out that nobody had drowned; it had been a false alarm, and I preached myself hoarse to a massive crowd for about an hour.

When we did the same drama in Reno, Nevada, two police cars suddenly pulled up and two policeman came rushing up to me. One of them pointed at the sheet-covered corpse and demanded, *"What've you got under there?"* I said, "A corpse. . .I'll resurrect her for you. Little maid, I say to you "Arise"' Fortunately, the teenage corpse sat up on cue and smiled. The cop burst into laughter and walked off mumbling, *"You guys can carry on. . ."* When we did it in Salt Lake City, I found myself preaching outside a Punk Rock joint. We had just gathered a good crowd when an ambulance pulled up, then a fire engine and police cars. I was able to stay calm as a policeman pulled me to one side, as it was the ninth time the police had joined in the drama. In a rather firm voice, he too asked what was going on. When I explained what we were doing, he said, *"Well, your little drama has just cost Salt Lake City one thousand bucks!"* Someone had seen us carrying the corpse, thought we had the real thing, and called the emergency department!

Why is it that humanity has to lose a loved one before they stop for a moment and ask what life is about? I have spoken in numbers of universities to so-called radicals, and these pseudo-intellectuals know the answer to everything except the issues that really matter. They can tell you what the moon is made of, but they haven't the faintest idea what they are doing here on earth. To them, our origin is a mystery. They know what they are made *of*, but they don't know what they were made *for*, or what death holds in store for them. Stupid questions such as, "Which came first, the chicken or the egg?" wouldn't even need to be asked if blind humanity opened the Bible to Genesis 1. The Bible tells us that the chicken beat the egg. Napoleon was right when he said, "Man will believe anything, as long as it's not in the Bible."

THE IMMACULATE ASSUMPTION
We embrace absurd speculations such as Darwin's Theory of Evolution without question. Humbling though it is, I must confess that I was once a Darwinist. I too sat in front of a television and nodded my unthinking head at evolution. I too listened as messy-haired, long-worded

scientists told me fact after fact without an ounce of substantiation. In truth, these imaginative dreamers merely got together with clever creative cartoonists to give us their dreams in drawing form. Face it, there are no facts to back up the theory tale. Listen to their special language, "We believe, surmise, suspect, think, assume, perhaps, maybe, possibly. . ." Darwin himself, whose theory has been twisted by evolutionists, could hardly believe how the world latched on to his speculation. "I was a young man with unformed ideas. I threw out queries, suggestions, wondering all the time over everything; and to my astonishment the ideas took like wildfire. *People made a religion out of them!*" Good choice of words. All you need to be a believer in the religion of evolution is blind faith. Just take everything you are taught about the assumption to be gospel truth.

Look at this newspaper report: "The study of man's origins have been thrown into turmoil by the discovery that human beings are almost genetically identical to chimpanzees and gorillas. The finding made by biologists overturns the accepted idea that mankind developed separately from apes in the distant past more than 20 million years ago, and have thus developed into very different creatures. The biologists say that the separation took place far more recently -- about five million years ago. Our ancestry is dramatically shorter than we once supposed, they believe. "We used to think we were cousins of the apes," says Professor David Pilbeam, a Harvard University anthropologist. "Now it is becoming more clear that we are more like brothers and sisters.""

What did he say, that we are *more like brothers and sisters to apes!* What an insult to apes. I have heard experts say that violence is unknown among them; gorillas are gentle creatures. They don't need to be continually policed so that they don't hate, rape, and murder like progressive man.

Maybe your faith rests on scientific proof, such as carbon dating. *Time* magazine's article in the science section of the June 11th edition 1990, subtitled "Geologists show that carbon dating can be way off," should show you how firm the ground is on which you stand.

PIGS HAVE PIGS

Not too many believers have looked closely at the theory. If they did, they would find that the structural pillars are either non-existent or very weak to say the least. "Nebraska man" was scientifically built up from one tooth, which was later found to be the tooth of an extinct pig. "Java" ape-man (found early this century) was nothing more than a piece of skull, a fragment of thigh bone and three molar teeth. The rest was the work of the imagination and plaster of paris. "Heidelberg man" was built up from a jawbone, a large chin section and some teeth. Most scientists of the day rejected it as being similar to the jawbone found in modern man. Yet stubborn evolutionists' jawbones have proven to be larger, as they have told us that this granddaddy is 250,000 years old. "Neanderthal man" came on the scene in 1856. He grew from a skull that is now known to be human. After "Piltdown man" celebrated his 500,000th birthday, his skull turned out to belong to that of a modern ape. All evidence of "Peking man," who was said to have been around at the time of his friend and neighbor, "Piltdown," has completely disappeared. "New Guinea" man dates way back to 1970, while it's been said of "Cro-magnon man," "One of the earliest and best established fossils is at least equal in physique and brain capacity to that of modern man" (small brain). . . *in other words there's no difference.*

Listen to this quote from a television program on the subject of evolution: "To make any kind of judgment, one has to appreciate how little evidence there is of all our ideas of human evolution. . .if we were to gather all the material on early human remains, from everywhere on earth, and bring it together in one place, it would scarcely fill a single coffin. . .there would be room to spare. . .the gaps are still huge. The missing "link" is more like a missing chain, stretching back longer than the period for which we had human fossils." Read the quote again. Look at what they are saying - "little evidence," "ideas," "scarcely fill a coffin." Again, well chosen words; put the idea in a coffin where it belongs and bury it forever. G.K. Chesterton was so right when he said, "The evolutionists seem to know everything about the missing link, except that it is missing."

Quite frankly, I can hardly believe that I once was a believer in such unfounded fables. The reason I agreed was that it wasn't very important whether it was true. As a Christian, however, the subject of origins now matters greatly to me because if evolution is true, the Bible is utterly false. Modern evolutionary theory (as opposed to Darwin's original theory), says that man was once an ape.

But the Bible says that there is one kind of flesh for man and one kind of flesh for animals. Modern evolution says man evolved from the ape, while the Bible says that every animal brings after its own kind. Dogs have puppies, not kittens. Cats have kittens, not chickens. Horses have foals, not calves. It doesn't matter how many thousands of years pass, elephants don't have giraffes, nor do monkeys have men. Every animal brings forth "after its kind."

It is interesting to note that pig valves are used as a replacement for human valves. Pig skin has even been grafted to deal with severe burns. In fact, pig tissues are the nearest in chemical composition to those of men. Perhaps wishful evolutionists should spend more time around the pig sty.

If evolution is true, then the Bible is not the Creator's revelation to humanity. In the negative, it means that man has no ultimate purpose in life, but on the positive side, it means neither is he ultimately responsible to any higher government other than what he places over himself. Therefore, "Let us eat and drink and be merry, for tomorrow we die" is life's philosophy. You and I may embark upon *any* sinful pleasure our heart desires *without fear of retribution*. It means we can ignore conscience completely and sin with reckless abandon -- clearly the erroneous philosophy of this generation.

CHAPTER 11
A PULLED PLUG

The incredible thing about God's promises is that they are not just "dead letter." God backs them up with His Holy Spirit to show us that He means what He says. Just as the producers of electricity could back up their instructional handbook with the fact that you can see the reality of their product by experiencing an electric shock, so God's promises carry a punch with them. Refuse to believe in electricity? Take a fork and put it in the electrical outlet. Suddenly you are a believer, because you have experienced the power.

The Bible tells us that when the gospel is preached, it comes in "power, in the Holy Ghost, and in much assurance." The reason you can walk around on God's earth, breathing God's air, seeing God's flowers, His birds, His trees, His sun, and not be aware of *Him*, is because you are spiritually dead. You are like an appliance with the plug pulled out.

We are actually made up of three parts: body, soul, and spirit. The body is the machine we walk around in; it is fearfully and wonderfully made. Our soul is our self-conscious part -- the area of the emotions, the will, and the conscience. But our spirit is our *God-conscious* part. You are not aware of God because your receiver is dead. That's why I went for 22 years without giving God two seconds of serious thought. My reasoning about eternity was merely in a natural realm. I was completely "without understanding." Yet from the moment I was plugged in, on the 25th of April, 1972, I have been utterly aware that "in Him we live and move and have our very being."

NO GREATER INSULT

The key that unlocks the door of salvation is faith. Without faith it is impossible to please God. Try having a relationship with someone and see if you can establish any sort of friendship without faith. Walk up to some girl and tell her your name. When she tells you hers, say, "I don't believe you." Watch her reaction. When she tells you where she lives, say that you don't believe that either. Carry on like that for a while, and before long you may be nursing a black eye. Your lack of faith in her is a strong insinuation that she is a liar. The command of Scripture is, "Have faith in God." If a meaningful human relationship can't be established without faith, what sort of relationship do you expect to have with God, if by your unbelief, you continue to call Him a liar?

Martin Luther said, "What greater insult can there be to God. . .than not to believe His promises!"

HOW DOES HE GET IN THE BOX?

Don't let reason destroy your faith. Imagine you had never seen a television set. As you look at your first, your hand runs across the smooth glass screen. "Push the button and you will see a person reading the news," I say with an air of pride at the miracle of modern technology. You smile and ask, "How does he get in there?" "Well, he's not exactly in the box." Your smile broadens as you ask, "Is he in there or isn't he?" "You don't understand. . .what happens is that unseen television waves are transmitted through the air. They are then picked up by what is called an aerial or receiver and sent down wires through electrical impulses into this plug, along this wire, and into the set."

The tone of your voice changes. "Listen. Do you expect me, a rational, logical human being, to believe that this "news reader" of yours floats invisibly through the air until he comes to your aerial, slides down the thing, through those wires, up the power point and into this box to read the news? Come on, what do you take me for, a fool!!" I smile and say, "I know it sounds fantastic, but all you have to do to prove what I say, is to push the button. The set will automatically come on." Despite the fact that your logic makes me seem like a fool, there is an air of confidence in my voice *because what I have said is provable!*

There is no denial; the claim of Christianity is truly fantastic. It maintains that the invisible God of Creation can supernaturally reveal Himself to you. Despite the fact that it is illogical, I have more than an air of confidence *because what I am saying is provable!* May I say, with all due respect, stop tapping the screen in skepticism. Push the button -- if you dare. I know that you can offer me a hundred reasons why it shouldn't work, *but push the button*. Do you have you an ulterior motive? Perhaps it's not that you *can't* find God, but *won't*. If you refuse to reach out and press the button of "repentance towards God and faith toward our Lord Jesus Christ," then you are choosing to remain in "wilful ignorance of the truth."

FOOD FOR THOUGHT
As I have said, the alternative to faith is paranoia. I have put together the following thoughts to illustrate the insanity of a world that refuses to have faith in God:

"My name is General Commonsense. The following is an intelligence report directly from the Battle of Tastebuds:

At present the battle scene is intense; but we must hold our ground. We must not lose Tastebuds. That hill was given to us, it is rightfully ours. To let it go would be nothing short of tragedy. In recent days, there has been relentless bombardment. In fact, Tastebuds is pitted with intense artillery assaults. When Hyper-health began peace talks years ago, I suspected that they secretly wanted to destroy Tastebuds. Now, my concern is that our troops will lose heart and hand it to them on a plate. They can handle the gunfire, but the enemy is flooding the troops with radio broadcasts and air dropped leaflet propaganda.

YOU ARE WHAT YOU EAT
The following is just a taste of the sort of stuff they are feeding us:

Whatever you do, don't eat white bread. In fact drop from

your diet anything made with refined flour; i.e., bread, rolls, pizzas, cakes, and the like. Be warned - fast foods are killing millions. Be careful when eating brown bread because much of it is actually dyed. Remember, cheese will cause cholesterol trouble. Don't just be concerned with *what* you eat, but *when* you eat. Cholesterol problems may be coming from the good old "three meals a day." Recent studies in an experimental group of people who ate 16 meals a day, showed that by having many small portions of food, they were more likely to have less cholesterol. Don't eat white sugar (aptly named *white death*) -- it's poisonous! Raw sugar is also refined. Don't drink soda pops, they contain coloring and preservatives. In fact most foods on sale in supermarkets contain colorings and preservatives. *Stay away from them.*

Keep in mind the fact that milk causes cholesterol. Coffee causes pancreatic cancer. It's been proven that tea has addictive properties. By the way, don't trust so-called "decaffeinated" coffee; studies have just discovered that it is *worse* for you than regular coffee. Milk products such as butter and cream cause cholesterol problems. Whatever you do. . .don't salt your food -- salt hardens the arteries! Bear in mind that a leading magazine warned, "Man realized from his earliest days that he had to have salt or perish; for without it the delicate water balance in the body is upset, *and death occurs through dehydration.*" So make sure you get enough salt. In fact, "Dr. David McCarron, co-head of the Division of Nephrology and Hypertension at Oregon Health Sciences University, warns that widespread salt restriction may actually harm more people than it helps." (*Reader's Digest,* Jan. '89)

Be careful when it comes to margarine, it's not a natural product. It actually contains antioxidants and food coloring. In fact, check out *Time*, August 27, 1990 under the health section - "Even margarine may be bad for the heart." Care also needs to be taken with alcohol, yoghurt, bread, and other yeast products; according to a Canadian study, these contain traces of cancer-causing "urothain." Also, roughage should be another area of concern. Make sure you get enough (*although too much can cause serious intestinal damage!*) Don't forget that it has been long known that your body does need a certain amount of cholesterol to survive ". . .The idea that cholesterol is "bad" is seriously flawed, since the chemical is produced naturally in the body, and is vital to the functioning of human cells" (*Time*). *So despite the alarm over the issue, keep the level of cholesterol constant.* Bear in mind this following thought from *Science Digest*, "Medical researchers have linked a new type of cholesterol to heart attacks. `We may have finally explained why up to twenty-five percent of men under sixty are prone to heart attacks for no apparent reason', says Cornell hematologist Katherine Haiiar. Certain people with a genetic disposition produce lipoprotein in large amounts, she explains, *and it can't be controlled with diet. . ."* Remember that.

Scientists have discovered that saccharin causes cancer in rats. Of course, you must be aware that eggs cause cholesterol problems. Did you know that *Time* (Nov. 21, 1988) reported, "The high cholesterol counts that have given ordinary eggs their bad reputation *may have been wrong to begin with."* Because of the controversy, you should still stay away from eggs. Stay clear of meat, it rots in your stomach. Besides, it's cruel to kill animals.

If you do become a vegetarian, take care not to eat vegetables or fruit that has been sprayed by pesticides. *U.S. News* reported that *390,000 tons* of pesticides are sprayed on crops and fruits each year in the United States alone! Be careful what water you drink. Much of today's water contains fluoride. . . *and we all know what that can do!* Never eat an apple after a meal. Dentists have released a report warning that apples contain natural sugars *that can rot your teeth.* Take care when eating wheat germ, muesli, carob and other so-called health products, only time will prove what they do to the body. Enjoy your food. Whatever you do, don't worry; *worry leads to hypertension, one of today's greatest killers!!*

A WORD FROM THE TOP

Some of the troops have swallowed the "You are what you eat" thing and have refused their weekly ration of nuts. However, I've just heard that a number of our most faithful officers have been studying the War Manual, and they have sent a wire giving instructions from it to the troops. It is so contrary to what they have been led to believe by the enemy. Some of the men are said to be in a state of shock. The wire reads, "Luke 14:34 - "Salt is good" " STOP Job 6:6 -Job salted his eggs STOP - Land "flowing with milk" God's blessing, not cursing STOP Meat given to eat, 1 Timothy 4 STOP - Worry big killer STOP Listen to Commonsense."

The War Manual comes straight from Headquarters. If the men will only trust the Manual, faith will replace their concern, and courage will conquer their fears.

It is near the midnight hour. Must sign off. - General Commonsense.
INTELLIGENCE 4U2C

CHAPTER 12
BENEVOLENT JELLY

It was August, 1972. An antique Gestetner sat in my office. I didn't even know what a "Gestetner" was until that day. It looked like a legless lawn-mower with a handle on one side. George, a 91-year-old Presbyterian minister, had heard of my conversion and insisted on buying one for me. He was really adamant, to a point where he parted with his $90 gladly.

A friend told me how to work the thing. It was just a matter of punching a stencil with an ordinary typewriter, placing the stencil over an ink-barrel, turning the handle, and it was supposed to print. I did as I was told, and to my surprise, it worked. Out the other end came the printed page.

My first tract was about South Africa. Right from the time I became a Christian, the issue concerned me. The whole world seemed intent on pointing a "holier than thou" finger at the sins of South Africa. I bounced off a hit song that went something like, "What we need is a great big melting pot. . .big enough to take the world and all its got; keep it stirring for a hundred years or more, and bring out coffee-colored people by the score." Even as a baby

Christian, I could see that the problem in South Africa wasn't the skin color. If one segregates the whites from the blacks, there's still rape and murder. If one integrates the society, the skin color just sparks off the hatred that is already in the human heart. The heart of man is at the heart of man's problems. The Soviet leader of the sixties, Kruschev, knew this. He said, "The chief failure with communism is its inability to create a new man." He was right. Communism says, "A new coat for every man," while Jesus Christ says, "A new man in every coat."

If I didn't like the way pigs lived, I could take a pig, scrub it clean, put deodorant under its pig-pits, and place it in a clean, thick-carpeted room. In a few days, however, the place would be a pig-sty. The only way to change a pig is to change its nature. The same applies to man. Politics cannot change the heart of man; history proves that. The only one who can change the human heart is Almighty God. When the appliance breaks down, take a look at the Instruction Book. The Book says sin is the cause of all human suffering, and Jesus Christ is the cure.

That was the message of the first tract we ever put together. A Christian brother saw it and ordered 5,000, much to the dismay of my right arm. It wasn't long before we sold the man-handled lawn-mower and had our tracts printed by a more modern means which, thanks to God, have run into the millions. It seems as fast as our ministry has grown, so has man's incredible ability to blame the symptoms rather than the cause. He insists on saying that money is the root of all evil, when it's not. The Bible says, "The *love* of money is the root of all evil." He prefers to pass the buck when the buck is his. How can money, mere paper, be evil? It is greed, lust for wealth and power, that is evil. America doesn't have a drug problem, it has a people problem. It's *people* that abuse drugs. Rarely does man say his problem is with man himself. He will always blame someone else. I know, because I did three and a half years hard labor as a pastor, listening to husbands blame wives and wives blame husbands while counseling marriage problem cases. If it's not someone else's fault, then it must be *God's* fault. Remember when God caught Adam in his rebellion, Adam said, "The woman which *you* gave to me. . ." It was either the woman, or it was God, but it wasn't Adam. A godly person will always justify God, while a guilty person will always try to justify himself. Insurance companies sum it up. When they have a disaster and no-one to blame, they call it "an act of God."

LET SLEEPING DOGS LIE

Look at the way dogs cross the road. The dog will wander onto a freeway with a "mind-on-the-wander" expression. The tail wags as he steps between cars without a second thought. Cars twist and turn as tires scream. The noise is deafening as vehicles smash into each other. The sleepy dog stops wagging his tail for a moment and looks at the pile of smoldering, broken cars on the freeway. His expression betrays his thoughts. His bone-burying brain doesn't equate for one moment that he is responsible for the disaster.

When man wanders onto the freeway of sin, his tail wags with delight. He thinks that this was what he was made for. His thoughts of any repercussion for his actions are shallow. His mind wanders into lust, then predictably, *he* wanders onto the path of adultery. Suddenly a disaster sits before him. His marriage is shattered, his name is slurred, his children are twisted and scarred; but like the dumb dog, he doesn't equate for one moment that *he* is solely responsible for his sin. As far as he is concerned, he had reason to do what he did. Bonebrain.

Perhaps you have genuine difficulties with Christianity. Maybe you are "almost persuaded to become a Christian." It could be that you are biblically misinformed through books you have read or because of what you have been told. Whatever the case, let's take a look at some of the most common objections to the Christian faith and see if we can clear them from your vision.

First, let's pry into the private life of one of our ancestors. It seems that the entire non-Christian world wants to know the details of where Cain got his wife. I will resist the temptation to say, "I would tell you if I was Abel." Cain simply married a distant sister, as you have, if you are a married man. God told Adam and Eve to be "fruitful and multiply." That doesn't mean they were to get into gardening and math. They were commanded by God to have children. No doubt they joyfully obeyed. We don't know how long it was until Cain took a wife, but you put two rabbits together (male and female) and even if you don't encourage them to mate, you will have a plague of rabbits before you know it. Those who yell *"Incest!"* should realize that when there is no law, there is no transgression. No doubt their offspring would have been in complete health, having God's blessing.

Maybe you've thought, "You can't tell me that a loving God will send innocent African natives to Hell *merely because they don't believe in Him!*" I totally agree with you. God won't send innocent natives to Hell merely because they don't believe in Him. They will go to Hell for murder, rape, lust, pride, hatred, lying, stealing, kidnapping, cannibalism, anger, deceit, torture, greed, adultery, etc. God doesn't overlook sin because of skin color! The only covering offered for sin is the blood of Jesus Christ. Your next thought, "So you're saying that those who obey the Gospel will be saved, and those who can't because they don't hear it, will go to Hell?" On Judgment Day, God will do what is right. The Bible says, "And how will they believe on Him if they have not heard? And how will they hear without a preacher?" If you *really* care for the heathen, get right with God yourself, then take them the good news of the forgiveness in Christ. Or is it closer to the truth that you couldn't care less about "innocent African natives," *and all you really want is to find an excuse to hold onto your sins?*

What about all the suffering in the world? Surely that's evidence that the Bible is wrong in saying that God is love.

God is not just one great big piece of benevolent jelly. He is not smiling at the human race. In fact, the Bible says that He is full of fury. The day is coming when He will "render His anger with fury and His rebuke with flames of fire." There are a few things in this area I don't understand, but that doesn't upset me too much. The day will come when I will "understand all things"; in the meantime I will trust God and use the understanding I do have to keep me going.

What I do understand is this: the Scriptures tell us that God's "judgments are in the earth," that He does hold back rain, send lightnings and cause earthquakes. I really don't know which, of the estimated million earthquakes each year, are merely workings of nature or actual judgments of God. When I look at "God-forsaken" countries like Ethiopia, I know that they need rain. God alone gives and withholds rain. Then I look at America. I see the richness of the land and the fatness of the people and say, "Dear God, it is true that you haven't treated *us* according to our sins. If You did, we would be like Ethiopia. Although I don't understand your mercies. . .I *am* grateful for them."

A little boy once said to his Mom, "I am sick of the food you keep giving me - potatoes, carrots, spinach. . .yuk! From now on, I choose my own diet. I am having nothing but chocolate candy bars for breakfast, lunch and supper!" Imagine what the kid would look like if he was allowed to eat what he wanted. His face would break into pimples. He may become very sick and even die because of a lack of proper food. His facial condition would be an evident token that he was on the wrong diet. . .even though it tastes good to him, it's not good *for* him.

Man's attitude is, "God, from now on, I don't want your diet. . .I want mine!" He chooses sin rather than righteousness; he wants what *tastes* good rather than what *is* good. As a direct result of humanity's sinful diet, painful pimples have broken forth throughout the whole face of the earth. There are diseases, floods, earthquakes, starvation, endless suffering and death. *All these things should show us that something is radically wrong with our diet.* Instead of using the sufferings of humanity as an excuse to reject God, see them as stark evidences to accept Him. They are very real reminders that what God says in the Bible is true. If we throw out the pilot because we want to take over the controls, we shouldn't moan when the plane heads for disaster.

CHAPTER 13
THE REAL THING

Perhaps the greatest hinderance to souls coming to Christ is the blatant hypocrisy within Christianity. Maybe your argument goes like this, "The Church is full of hypocrites, and besides, *nothing has caused more wars in history than religion!*" No argument there. But let's take a close look at what a hypocrite is. The word actually means "pretender." In other words, the hypocrite is not a Christian, he is a *pretending* Christian. He is a non-Christian pretending to be a Christian. . .he's not on our side, *he's on yours!*

THE GENUINE ARTICLE
The way U.S. federal agents train their officers to recognize counterfeit bills is to have them study the genuine article. When they see the false, they spot it because their eye is trained to know the real thing.

The real thing in Christianity is someone who is faithful, kind, loving, good, without hypocrisy, gentle, humble, patient, self-controlled, and he will speak the truth in love. So next time you're watching T.V., and see a black-hatted, Abraham Lincoln-style bearded, booze-sodden, Old-

English speaking, Bible-quoting hypocrite plunge a pitchfork into his neighbor's back "in the name of the Lord," ask to yourself, Could this be a *genuine Christian?* Does he love his neighbor as himself? Is he kind, gentle, good, generous, self-controlled? Does he love his enemies? Does he do good to those who despitefully use him? If not, then you have another hypocrite, pretending to be a Christian. Nothing new. Non-Christians caused the first world war, the second world war, the Korean war, the Vietnam war, and what's worse, they're still causing wars *in the name of God.* When the Faulkland Islands crisis broke out, the British said, "God is with us.," So did the Argentineans. Americans are well versed in "Praise the Lord, and pass the ammunition." The Nazis had "Got mit uns" (God with us) engraved on their belt buckles. No, one doesn't have to go to Church to see the hypocrite. In fact, the best place to look for the hypocrite is in the mirror. Who of us can say he or she has been forever free from pretense? The hypocrite is the teenager who is pure of eyes in front of parents, but burns with lust in the heart. The hypocrite is the businessman who is slick and clean, smooth and polished, signing his letters "Yours sincerely," but cutting his client's throat for a fast buck. The hypocrite is she who is the virtuous spouse, but feasts her covetous heart on the adulteries of the soap operas. Hypocrisy is having "In God we trust" on our money, when it is nothing but a pretence. Hypocrites sing, "God bless America," yet use that Holy Name to curse. Hypocrites are those whose pilgrim fathers established "one nation under God," but give homage to a stone idol, a goddess of liberty, spending literally millions on a face-lift, saying, "She is a light to the world. . .she has given us freedom." Hypocrisy is the pretense of concern for the health of cigarette smokers, warning on advertisements of the fatal effects of tobacco and reaping $32,000,000,000 in revenue each year from the drug at the same time. Yet hundreds of thousands of Americans die as a direct result of cigarette smoking each year. Hypocrisy is a society that says it cares for children, yet murders millions in the womb. The hypocrite can see sin in South Africa, but never in himself. If the whole world hates a hypocrite, what must God think of him. All hypocrites will go to Hell. If the hypocrite so offends you, you won't want to spend eternity in Hell with him, will you?

If your whole life (including your secret thoughts and deeds) was made public, would you be one who is free of pretense in the sight of the world? If the press of America had access to your every secret, could you run for political office, or would you find yourself in the headlines of *The National Enquirer?*

Be careful when you judge others. We can often make tragic errors, when we pass a quick conclusion and say that someone is a hypocrite. I try to walk with a discerning mind but keep free from a judgment that is quick to condemn. If we don't have the truth, the whole truth and nothing but the truth, we can judge someone guilty when in reality they are totally innocent. There is only One who has total truth about each of us and His judgment is, and will be, "according to righteousness."

KNOCK KNOCK
There is nothing as persistent as a spider. We were once plagued by large numbers of spider webs around our

home. It didn't matter how many times I got rid of them, the next morning there were brand new ones with snoozing, night-shift workers hiding somewhere nearby.

One day, I decided that my web-removing battles were being lost; so armed with a small stick in one hand and repellent in the other, I crept up to one web and gently knocked on it with the stick. I could almost hear the spider stirring from sleep and mumbling, "Good - breakfast!" With Daniel, my youngest, cleverly imitating the sound of a distressed pre-breakfast fly, the spider didn't stand a chance. Out he sprung from his hiding place and rushed into the middle of his web. For a split second, one could see that his facial expression resembled that of an Oscar-winning actor caught in a surprise attack of the enemy. Then, before he could retreat, without mercy, I blasted him with the repellent.

Instead of dealing with the symptom, I had gone for the cause. If we are ever to deal with the plaguing problems of humanity, mankind must do the same. His persistent and painful predicaments are clearly the web. I don't need to show it to you, just watch the television news tonight or pick up your daily newspaper. The web of deceit, hatred, divorce, wife-beating, child-molestation, murder, greed, rape, assaults, incest, kidnapping, lust, adultery, terrorism, envy, etc., are spun across the whole earth. But where is the spider? Well he's hard to locate. He sleeps quietly, undiscovered by the human eye. How will we bring him into light? The stick of the Law of God is the only effective means of revealing him. If we are courageous enough to go through the Law, I'm sure his ugly head will appear just enough to see his hiding place. The grotesque beast has concealed himself within your heart. Later on, if you are willing, we will lure him out into the open, and with the help of God, spray him with the gospel-spray of the blood of Jesus Christ.

CHAPTER 14
WHO WROTE THE LETTER?

A few days after my conversion, I kept hearing my friend who had led me to Christ saying, "Ray Comfort, *a Christian!?*" He would shake his head and repeat the phrase. I was the last person in the world he thought would want to become a Christian. I had everything in the world. . .I was so happy, *I couldn't possibly be interested in everlasting life!* Little did he know. I had everything in the world, but I also knew that time would rip it from my hands. My happiness bubble was awaiting the sharp pin of reality.

Now, after my conversion, the pin had been dulled to a point of ineffectuality. Suddenly, the Bible fascinated me. I read it with the fervor of a man gripped by gold fever. Well, was the Bible trustworthy? Could I believe what I read? Had it changed through the years, or was it full of mistakes, as is so often said?

When a man writes a letter, does *he* write it or does his pen? Obviously, he writes the letter, and the pen is the instrument he uses. The claim of the Bible is that it is *God* who did the writing, while men were the instruments He used to pen His Word to humanity. If the Bible is indeed the word of our Creator, and it claims that our greatest enemy, death, has been destroyed, then we would be fools not to at least give it a fleeting glance. But if it is merely an historical book, the writings of men, it needs to be exposed as fraudulent; as millions have been deceived by it.

The irony of the Christian faith is that it *seems* to be intellectual suicide, but proves to be the ultimate intellectual challenge.

In this chapter, we will look at four sets of amazing facts:
>1/ Scientific,
>2/ General,
>3/ Prophetic,
>4/ Politically prophetic.

Before we do, let's realize that the Bible was written by about 40 men, over a period of 1600 years, beginning at 1500 B.C. Its claim is that these men were inspired by God (2 Peter 1:21). If this is correct, this should be no ordinary book. In the light of these thoughts, let's look at the following:

SCIENTIFIC FACTS:

1/ At a time when science taught that the earth sat on a foundation of either a large animal or a giant (1500 B.C.), the Bible spoke of the earth's free float in space, "He. . .hangeth the earth upon nothing" (Job 26:7).

2/ When twentieth-century man has just begun to understand the existence of the ozone layer (an invisible shield that protects the earth from the harmful rays of the sun), the Bible mentioned it in 800 B.C. "The shields of the earth belong unto the Lord" (Psalm 47:9).

3/ The ancient Book of Job (3,500 years old) also reveals the fact that the moon doesn't shine - "Behold even the moon, and it shineth not. . ." (Job 25:5). This wasn't discovered until 3,000 years later when the telescope revealed that it is merely reflecting the light of the sun.

4/ The Bible also tells us in Isaiah 40:22 that the earth is round - "It is He who sitteth upon the circle of the earth." Secular man discovered this 2400 years later.

5/ The Book of Job is very specific in its description of light saying, "Where is the way where light dwells" (Job 38:19). Modern man has only just discovered that light has a "way," involving motion traveling at 186,000 miles per second.

6/ Not too many people realize that radio waves and light waves are two different forms of the same thing. God told this fact to Job in the year 1500 B.C., "Canst thou send lightnings, that they may go and say unto thee, Here we are?" Who would have believed that light could be sent and actually speak? This was first realized in 1864 when "the British scientist James Clerk Maxwell suggested that electricity and light waves were two forms of the same thing" (*Modern Century Illustrated*

Encyclopedia Vol. 12).

7/ Science has now discovered that stars send out radio waves. These are received on earth as a high pitch. God mentioned this in Job 38:7 . . .when the morning stars sang together. . ."

8/ When science is in the dark as to why the dinosaur disappeared, the Bible would seem to shed light on the subject. In Job 40:15-24, God Himself speaks, describing the largest of all the creatures He made. He speaks of this massive animal as being herbivorous (plant-eating), having its strength in its hips, a tail like a large tree, very strong bones, a habitat among trees, able to consume large amounts of water, and being of great height. Then the Scriptures say, ". . .He who made him can make his sword to approach unto him." In other words, God brought extinction to this huge prehistoric creature.

9/ "Most cosmologists (scientists who study the structure and evolution of the universe) agree that the Genesis account of creation, in imagining an initial void, may be uncannily close to the truth." (*Time,* Dec. 1976).

10/ Science expresses the universe in five terms: time, space, matter, power and motion. The Book of Genesis Chapter One revealed such truths to the Hebrews in 1450 B.C. "In the beginning (time) God created the Heaven (space) and the earth (matter). . .And the Spirit (power) of God moved (motion) upon the face of the waters." Science is slowly coming into line with the Bible.

MORE AMAZING FACTS
Let's now look at some more amazing points:

GENERAL FACTS
1/ In Genesis Chapter 6, God gave Noah the dimensions of the one million, three hundred thousand cubic square foot ark he was to build. In 1609 at Hoorn in Holland, a ship was built after that same pattern, and this revolutionized shipbuilding. By 1900 every large ship on the high seas was definitely inclined towards the proportions of the ark (as verified by "Lloyd's Register of Shipping" in the *World Almanac*).

2/ God asked Job a strange question in Job 38:22, "Hast thou entered into the treasures of the snow?" This didn't make too much sense to us until the advent of the microscope, revealing the incredible beauty of snow crystals.

3/ In the Book of Beginnings, in Genesis Chapter 16, God said that Ishmael (the progenitor of the Arab race, see *Time*, April 4, 1988) would be a "wild man, and every man's hand will be against him; and he shall dwell in the presence of all his brethren." Four thousand years later, who could deny that this prophecy is being fulfilled in the

Arab race? The Arabs and the Jews are "brethren" having the same ancestors. The whole cause of Middle-east conflict is because they are dwelling together.

4/ Two prophecies (Genesis 49:1 & 20, Deuteronomy 33:24), written around 3,000 years B.C., combine to tell us, "In the latter days. .Asher. .let him dip his foot in oil." As one studies a map of the tribe of Asher, it perfectly resembles a foot poised to dip. In 1935 the Great International Iraq Petroleum Enterprise opened precisely at the base of the foot, pumping a million gallons of oil a day to the Haifa harbor.

5/ In Isaiah 66:7 & 8 (700 B.C.), the Prophet gives a strange prophecy, "Before she travailed, she brought forth; before her pain came, she was delivered of a man-child; who hath heard such a thing? Who hath seen such things? Shall the earth be made to bring forth in one day? Or shall a nation be born at once? For as soon as Zion travailed, she brought forth her children." In 1922 the League of Nations gave Great Britain the mandate (political authority) over Palestine. On May 14, 1948, Britain withdrew her mandate, and the nation of Israel was "born in a day." There are more than 25 Bible prophecies concerning Palestine that have been literally fulfilled. Probability computer estimations conclude that the chances of these being accidentally fulfilled are more than one chance in 33 million.

6/ In 1905, Scotland Yard in England launched into a new era of scientific detection. At a murder trial, Detective Inspector Stockley Collins explained to the jury that skin patterns could provide up to 20 characteristics on a single finger. Over 10 years, he had examined a million fingerprints and never found more than three identical characteristics on the fingers of any two people. They discovered that every single man has a seal, an imprint on his hand, which can show other men crimes he has committed. The Book of Job tells us this amazing fact many thousands of years before Scotland Yard discovered it. "He (God) sealeth up the hand of every man, that all men may know his work" (Job 37:7).

7/ In spring of 1947, the Dead Sea Scrolls were discovered. These manuscripts were copies of large portions of the Old Testament, a thousand years older than any other existing copies. Study of the scrolls has revealed that the Bible hasn't changed in content down through the ages as many skeptics had surmised.

Many times I have heard the statement that the Bible is "full of mistakes." Over the years I have spent literally thousands of hours searching the Scriptures, and I can't find them. In fact, if you can prove to me that there is even one mistake in the Word of God, I will give you $500 cash.

CHAPTER 15
DEATH SENTENCE FOR ERROR

PROPHETIC FACTS

Bible Law states that if a prophet was not 100 percent accurate in his prophecy, he was to be put to death. Nostradamus (the occultic prophet), who was 70 percent correct in his predictions would have been stoned to death as a false prophet. If the Bible is the Book of the Creator, its prophecies will be perfectly accurate. Now bear in mind the faultless description the Bible gives of this day and age in which we live (the "latter days"), as we look at the "signs of the times." These signs are to warn us of the coming Day when Almighty God reveals Himself to humanity; when His Kingdom comes to earth, and His will is done on earth "as it is in Heaven."

1/ False Bible teachers will be money hungry, be smooth talkers, have many followers, and will slur the Christian faith (2 Peter 2:1-3).

2/ Homosexuality will be increasingly evident at the end of the age (2 Timothy 3:3). There are reported to be 17,000,000 homosexuals in the U.S. alone.

3/ Earthquakes will increase (Matthew 24:7). Science estimates that there are a million earthquakes each year, with up to twenty going on simultaneously at any moment.

4/ There will be increasing heart attacks resulting in death (Luke 21:26).

5/ Many wars will erupt (Matthew 24:6). There have been over 100 wars since 1945, with over 16 million deaths.

6/ Deadly diseases will be prevalent (Matthew 24:7). The former U.S. Surgeon-General C. Everett Koop confirmed estimations that 100,000,000 will die of Aids by 1997. 160,000 Americans die of cancer each year.

7/ People will forsake the Ten Commandments as a moral code, committing adultery, stealing, lying, and killing (Matthew 24:12). Recently there were 2300 murders in one year in the city of Los Angeles.

8/ There will be a cold, religious system denying God's power (2 Timothy 3:5).

9/ The Bible warns that these times will reveal much increase in the occult (1 Timothy 4:1). In the U.S. there is enough business to keep 10,000 full-time workers and 175,000 part-time astrologers working.

10/ Men will substitute fantasy in place of Christian

truth (2 Timothy 4:4). This is so evident at Christmas when the birth of the Savior is lost behind the myth of Santa Claus.

11/ The fact that God once flooded the earth (the Noahic flood) will be denied (2 Peter 3:5).

12/ There will be an increase in famines (Matthew 14:7).

13/ The institution of marriage will be forsaken (1 Timothy 4:3).

14/ Interest in vegetarianism will increase (1 Timothy 4:3).

15/ There will be a cry for peace (1 Thessalonians 5:3).

16/ Knowledge (Hebrew, "science") will greatly increase (Daniel 12:4).

17/ There will be hypocrites in the Church (Matthew 13:25-30).

18/ Stress will be part of living in the "latter days" (2 Timothy 3:1).

19/ There will be increase in religious cults (Matthew 24:11).

20/ There will be much intimidation from nation to

nation (Matthew 24:7).

21/ The future will seem fearful to many (Luke 21:26).

22/ Humanity will become very materialistic (2 Timothy 3:5).

23/ There will be many involved in travel (Daniel 12:4). In 1988 Americans spent approximately $32.9 billion on international travel.

24/ The Christian Gospel will be preached as a warning to all nations (Matthew 24:14).

25/ Christians will be hated (Luke 21:17).

26/ Many who profess to be Christians will fall away from their faith (Matthew 24:10).

27/ There will be "signs in the sun" (Luke 21:25). This is possibly a reference to sun spots which, according to the dictionary, are "dark, irregular spots appearing periodically on the sun's surface."

28/ There will be an increase in pestilence. In the U.S. 390,000 tons of pesticides are sprayed on crops each year (*U.S. News*, Nov. 16, '87).

29/ Youth will become rebellious (2 Timothy 3:2).

30/ Men will mock the signs of the end of the age

with this philosophy, "These signs have always been around." This will be because they fail to understand that God is not subject to the dimension of time (2 Peter 3:4).

The sign which is the culmination of all these signs will be the Israeli occupation of Jerusalem (Luke 21:14). In 1948 the Jews, after over 1900 years without a homeland, occupied Israel. In 1967 they set foot in Jerusalem fulfilling these words of Jesus Christ spoken 2,000 years earlier. God had warned that if the Jews forsook His Law, He would scatter them throughout the earth, allowing them to be put to shame, then draw them back to Israel (Jeremiah 3:3, Ezekiel 36:24). The Bible makes special reference to the Jews being drawn back to Israel from "the north country" (Jeremiah 23:7, 8). The nation of Israel is the night-light on the clock of Bible prophecy. It shows us how close we are to the "midnight hour."

POLITICALLY PROPHETIC FACTS:

RUSSIA AND ISRAEL

A number of books of the Bible speak of future events. Ezekiel 38 (written approx. 600 B.C.) prophesies that in these times, i.e. the "latter days" (vs. 16), Russia (referred to as the "Prince of Rosh," see *Smith's Bible Dictionary* Page 584), will combine with Iran, Libya (in Hebrew called "Put"), and Communistic Ethiopia (in Hebrew called "Cush") and attack Israel (vs. 5-8). This will take place after an Israeli peace initiative has been successful (vs. 11). The Bible even gives the Russian reasoning for and direction of the attack (vs. 10-15), as well as the location of the battle (Armageddon - Revelation 16:14). This is generally interpreted as meaning "the mountain of Megiddo" which is located on the north side of the plains of Jezreel. Russia is ready, "The Soviets are entrenched all around the rim of the Middle East heartland -- In Afghanistan, South Yemen, Ethiopia, and Libya" ("Countdown in the Middle East," *Reader's Digest,* May 1982).

It would seem from Scripture that nuclear weapons will be used in this battle, speaking of search parties looking for bones of those killed in the war. When the bone is located, it will not be touched, but "a marker" will be set by it; and it will be buried by special teams (Ezekiel 39:14-15), a more than possible reference to radio-active contamination. The Book of Joel (800 B.C.) also speaks of this war, confirming the nuclear weapon aspect with "pillars of smoke" being seen during the battle (Joel 2:30). It seems that it even speaks of flame-throwing tank warfare. Not having access to the word "tank," the prophet describes his vision of these war machines with, "A fire devours before them. . .they climb the wall. . .every one marches in formation. . .they run to and fro in the city . . .they run on the wall. . .the earthquakes before them" (Joel 2:3-10). By December, 1988, the Soviet Union had in its arsenal 41,000 tanks.

Israel will never have lasting peace until she obeys God. If she will obey God's statutes and keep His Commandments, He will give her rain in due season, an abundance of food, freedom from fear, victory over the enemy, and peace within the land (Leviticus 26:1-13).

Sadly, from what we see of Scripture, Israel will only seek God as a last resort when she sees that she cannot prevail against the might and power of the Russian invasion (Joel 2:12-20). Deuteronomy 4:30 gives warning that it would take tribulation to turn Israel to God in the "latter days." When Israel finally turns to God in true repentance, God will take pity on His people and remove far from them the "northern army" (Joel 2:20).

Another sign of the "latter days" will be a clear understanding of the judgments and the will of God (watch out for Iran and Iraq, known as "Persia" in scripture (Ezekiel 38:5). They will also have a part to play in waring against Israel during this time).

No other generation has seen Russia mustering forces against Israel, the Arab-Israeli conflict in the Middle East, and the Jews in Jerusalem. No other generation has had the scientific knowledge to help it understand "strange" scriptures, nor have they had access to the Bible as we have, so that we can understand perfectly the times in which we live. "The anger of the Lord will not turn back until He has executed and performed the thoughts of His heart. In the latter days you will understand this perfectly" (Jeremiah 23:20). Keep one eye on the Middle East. . .and the other towards the heavens.

CHAPTER 16
GOING FOR THE SPIDER

It's been said that the worst thing you can ever say to another human being is, *"You are wrong!"* It is a sad indictment on the human race that the statement is probably true. Even if the person is totally in the wrong, and you tell him so without discretion, you will more than likely alienate yourself from him with such a blow to his ego.

You may have picked up this book totally convinced that you were right in your beliefs. But as you read its pages, you began to see that there is another point of view; that in fact God is a reality, and that the Bible is indeed the Word of God. It is my hope that this revelation has come to you in a spirit of gentleness on my part, so that you won't feel alienated from me, because I want to speak from my heart to yours.

Imagine you and I are seated next to each other in a plane. I have very reliable information that the plane is about to crash. In fact, the whole aircraft is rocking and shaking to a point where it seems it may fall to pieces any moment. Still, I'm not too fearful, because I've reached under my seat, found a parachute and put it on. What concerns me is the fact that you don't see your need to put yours on! Even though you know you have to jump, you have three lines of argument as to why you should leave the parachute off. Firstly, you're adamant that the plane had no maker. Secondly, you have noticed that a number of the other passengers say they're wearing a parachute, when it's obvious to you that they are not. And thirdly, you haven't put it on because you think you can somehow defy the law of gravity.

I feel a bit embarrassed at having to point out to you that if the plane was made, there must be a maker. But after a while you see my reasoning. You also accept my answer to your second objection - that if the other passengers wanted to pretend they were wearing a 'chute, they would find out their mistake when they jumped. My suggestion to you was, best get yours on first, then see if you can persuade "pretenders." The third objection was also answered by simple logic. I found that the most effective way to convince you of your need, was to "hang you out the door of the plane by your ankles," so to speak. I feel at peace about having you put the parachute on for a motive of self preservation.

THE MAIN OBJECTIONS
Let's now swing from this allegory to real life. We will say that your two main objections as to why you shouldn't accept the Savior were,

> 1/ The question of the existence of God. Now you are convinced of His existence.
> 2/ Hypocrisy in the Church. Now you know that God will judge hypocrites; when they die, they will see their error.

108

Your problem now, is that you still somehow think that you don't *need* a savior - someone to stand on your behalf, an advocate for your defence before the Judge of the Universe. You think you can somehow defy the Law of God. *Please,* trust me for a moment, while I attempt to "hang you out the plane door by your ankles." It will be a fearful experience, but it is necessary. It should have the effect of helping you to see the seriousness of what I am trying to say.

My aim is not to convince you of the existence of a moral Law, you already know it exists. The Bible says that the "work of the law" is written on your heart, that God has given "light to every man." You have always known that it is wrong to steal, to lie, etc. - conscience has always been there as a judge on the courtroom of your mind, giving you knowledge of what is right and wrong since the time you can remember. No, my aim is to persuade you of the *consequences* of breaking that Law. To do this, all I require is for me to get a hold on the "ankles" of your honesty.

What we will do, is thoroughly go through the Ten Commandments to see if you have broken any of them. As we do so, remember these three facts:

    1/ God sees the sins of your youth, as though it were yesterday. Just as time doesn't forgive transgression of civil law (i.e. a murderer is still a murderer twenty years after the crime), so time doesn't forgive sin.

    2/ God sees your thought-life. He made the mind of man, so surely He can see what he made -

nothing is hid from His omniscient eye.

3/ He is perfect, just, good, holy and utterly righteous. By that, I mean, by His very nature, He *must* punish transgression. If He sees a murder take place, He must eventually bring the murderer to justice, something that the most dense of us can understand, even if there is disagreement on the *form* of punishment.

THE LAW

It is important to realize that being a Christian doesn't determine that you will live eternally; it just defines the *location*. If you die, as Jesus said, "in your sins," God will judge you accordingly. There is no place in Scripture for "purgatory," for a second chance.

The Bible reveals that you and I have failed to put God first, to love Him with heart, mind, soul and strength. It states plainly, "There is none that seeks after God; there is none that understand. . ." The First Commandment is to put God first in our affections. That's not an option, it's a command.

Imagine buying a child a toy for his pleasure, and having him love the toy more than he loved you. Yet isn't that what you've done with God? Didn't He shower the gift of life upon you; giving you freedom, food, family, eyes, ears, a mind to think with? And you used that mind to deny the existence of the One who gave you the mind in the first place! Isn't it true that you have been guilty of complete and utter ingratitude? If someone gave you a car as a gift, should you thank them? Have you ever humbly thanked

Him for the gift of life. If you have, but you've never obeyed His command to repent, then your "thanks" is nothing but empty hypocrisy.

If you love anything more than you love God, whether it is husband, wife, brother, sister, boyfriend, girlfriend, car, sport, or even your own life, you are loving the gift more than the Giver. What have you got that you didn't receive? Everything you have came to you via the goodness of God. Jesus said that we should so love God that all our other affections for mother, father, brother, and sister, should seem as "hate," compared to the love we have for the God who gave them to us. It has been said, if the greatest commandment is to love God with all our heart, mind, soul and strength, then the greatest sin, is failure to do so.

But more than that. The Bible says that the First Commandment also involves loving your neighbor as yourself. In the story Jesus gave of the Good Samaritan, the man picked up a beaten stranger, bathed his wounds, carried him to an inn, gave money for his care and said to the inn keeper that if he spent any more money while he was gone, he would pay his expenses. That is a picture of how God *commands* we should treat our fellow human beings. We should love them as much as we love ourselves. . .whether they be friend or foe. In fact Jesus didn't call that story the "good" Samaritan; he wasn't good, he merely carried out the basic requirements of the Law. Have you loved humanity as yourself? You be the judge; have you kept the Law? Will you be innocent or guilty on Judgment Day? I'm not judging you - I'm asking you to judge yourself. Sentence for transgression of the First Commandment is death.

The Second Commandment is, "You shall not make yourself a graven image" (you won't find this in the Roman Catholic Bible; it was taken out because it exposed idolatry within the church. What they did was to break the Tenth Commandment up into two, to make up for the one they deleted). This command means that we shouldn't make a god in our own image, either with our hands or with our minds. I was guilty of this. I made a god to suit myself. My god didn't mind lust, a fib here or there; in fact he didn't have *any* moral dictates. But in truth, my god didn't exist. He was a figment of my imagination, shaped to conform to my sins. Almost all non-christians have an idolatrous understanding of the nature of God.

Let me show you what I mean. Although the Bible says that humanity hates God without cause, most would deny that they do. You may not hate *your* god, but look at the Biblical revelation of our Creator: God killed a man in Genesis 38 because He didn't like his sexual activities. He commanded Joshua to kill every Canaanite man, woman and child, without mercy. He drowned the whole human race, but for eight people in the Noahic flood. He killed a man because he touched the Ark of the Covenant. He killed a husband and wife in the New Testament, because they told one lie! Now *that* God, says humanity, is not so easy to snuggle up against.

Before you ask why God killed a couple for telling a lie, ask "Why didn't God kill me, when I lied for the first time!" All God did was to treat them according to their sins. When we did wrong for the first time and didn't get struck by lightning, we then concluded that God didn't see or didn't care about what we did, and with that, became more bold in our sin. Yet, all that happened was that God extended His mercy toward you and I, that we might have a time of grace to repent.

If we caught a revelation of what God is really like, we would fall flat on our faces in terror. Just take an objective look at some of His natural laws. If you break electrical or gravitational laws, the consequences are fearful, but they are merely a weak shadow of the eternal moral Law of God. My words cannot express what God is like, but His Law gives us some insight into His holy nature. The Law reveals utter holiness, supreme righteousness, and absolute truth. God has a violent passion for justice.

What has your understanding of God been like? Do you tremble at the very thought of His power and holiness? Have you seen Him in the light of Holy Scripture, or have you made up a god to suit yourself? If that is the case, you are guilty of idolatry. The Law's sentence for idolatry is death, and according to Scripture, no idolater will enter the Kingdom of Heaven.

The Third Commandment is, "You shall not take the name of the Lord your God in vain. For the Lord will not hold him guiltless who takes His name in vain." I wonder if you have ever given any thought as to the origin of cursing. It's a rather strange thing, in that the words used to curse may be quite an inoffensive part of the English language. Take for instance "dam" and "hell." The words in themselves have legitimate meanings. However the *manner* in which they are used, determines whether or not they fit the category of curse words. Let's look at a few common words in use, and see if we can understand how they made it onto the pop chart of cursing. Firstly, the ever popular curse word, "bastard." In recent years, many have looked at wed-lock and come to the conclusion that any word which ends with the word "lock," is a little too binding, so they have chosen to keep the door open and live with someone without the vows of marriage. Consequently, many of today's children are in essence bastards. . .they are born out of wedlock. Yet despite the fact that illegitimacy no longer carries the social stigma it once had, bastard itself still has strong connotations to it. "You bastard!" still packs a powerful punch and makes it to number one on the insult/cursing charts.

This brings us to the second category we are going to look at, that of "circumstantial cursing." Take for instance Joe Average. Joe had a very restless night's sleep. He tossed and turned until the early hours of the morning, finally drifting off around 5 a.m. After being awakened by his alarm at 6.30 a.m., he feels *worse* than he did before he went to sleep. He burns his breakfast toast; the milk on the stove boils over, and as he gets in his car, he feels very close to boiling point himself. Never mind, at least he isn't late for work. He had set his alarm to go off just a little earlier than usual, because of the fact that he had arrived ten minutes late for work the previous day. His boss had given him such a dressing down, that he wanted to be early today. Upsetting the boss had been the reason for such a sleepless night. He sat is his car, paused for a moment and took a deep breath, to try and release his frustrations.

As he reached out and turned the key of the car, he sat in stunned unbelief. The battery gave a last, pathetic dying grunt. Joe's eyes bulged with rage. He gripped the steering wheel in an iron grip, and breathed out through gritted teeth, the internationally, ever popular curse word, "Sh-t!!!" He wanted to express utter disgust, and the word seemed to fit the situation as far as he was concerned. The reason for the use of these words to curse either a person or a situation, is reasonably obvious. However, the purpose in using what in respectable circles, is commonly called the "f" word, is a little more obscure.

Few would be unaware of the fact that the word is slang to describe the act of sexual intercourse. Using it as an insult/curse, in telling someone to "get f---ed," may arise from the fact that a person, many years ago, was punished by being sent to the stocks if they were caught in unlawful sex. Their crime was said to be "For Understanding Carnal Knowledge." The words have evolved over the years to mean more than they originally said. To express the desire for a fellow human being be in such a state, has grown to become a gross insult. In fact, the term is so offensive, it may get you arrested if used in a public place.

Despite the fact that Joe Average arrived twenty minutes late for work, he kept his job. But the *look* his boss had given him was worse than the verbal dressing down he had the day before. Joe knew he was skating on thin ice.

NOT EVEN A GROAN

Insomnia seemed to come in waves with Joe. Once again he had tossed and turned for what seemed like an eternity, before getting a few hours sleep. But this day, he was determined to make it to work on time. He needed to hang on to this job. To ensure this, he had a new battery put into the car, and set his alarm clock to go off even earlier. He felt confident that things would run more smoothly today. He even stood over the toaster to make sure the toast didn't burn. Making it to the other side of breakfast without mishap didn't seem to help his disposition one bit. Lack of sleep made him feel like a crystal vase waiting to be shattered.

As he sat in the car, he once again closed his eyes and took a deep breath, before heading out into the jungle of a packed freeway. He then confidently reached out his hand to turn the key. It took a few seconds for reality to sink in to his dulled brain. His ears couldn't believe what they weren't hearing. *There wasn't even a groan from his "brand new" battery!* For some reason it was dead. It was all too much for Joe. The vase shattered. Yesterday's curse word wasn't strong enough to express how he felt. Through gritted teeth, and with bulged eyes flaming, he spat out, *"Jesus Christ!"*

The question comes to mind as to why Joe should use the name of a person in that situation. It does seem to make some sense that he used an unclean word like sh-t to express disgust, but why use the name of Jesus Christ?

Why didn't he say, "Buddha!" or "Muhammad!" What's so special about the name of Jesus? To answer that question, we have to go to the only source of information on the subject, the Bible. In it we see that God has, "highly exalted Him (Jesus) and given Him a name that is above every name." According to the Bible, there is no other name on this earth that deserves honor and respect, than that of the name of Jesus Christ. When Joe used it in the way he did, he was substituting it for the word sh-t. *In other words, Joe aligns the Name with human excrement.* He counts them as the same thing. The Bible calls this "blasphemy," warning "the Lord will not hold him guiltless who takes His name in vain." In fact Jesus said, "The world hates me, because I testify of its deeds, that they are evil." What greater verbal expression of hatred can there be for someone, than to use their very name in such a context. Humanity doesn't even use the name of Hitler to curse. His name is not despised with the venomous hatred needed to qualify it for such use.

JUST A WORD

Most who use God's name in blasphemy would deny that they are using it in the way I have described. In fact, when they blaspheme, they will often say that they don't even know that they are doing it. To them it's "just a word." If that is your justification, *then your own mouth condemns you.* You so count the name of God as nothing, it passes by your lips without even registering in your mind - *you truly use it "in vain." Don't you realize what you are doing?* You are cursing the name of the very One who gave you life! Penalty under the Law for blasphemy is death.

The Fourth Commandment tells us, "Remember the Sabbath day, to keep it holy." I ignored this command for 22 years of my non-Christian life. Not for a second did I say, "God gave me life, *what does He therefore require of me?*" let alone set aside one day in seven to worship Him in spirit and in truth. Death is the sentence under the Law for Sabbath breaking.

A LONG LIFE
The Fifth is, "Honor Your Father and Mother." That means we are commanded to value them implicitly in a way that is pleasing in the sight of God. Have you *always* honored your parents in a way that's pleasing in God's sight? Have you always had a perfect attitude in all things towards them? Ask God to remind you of some of the sins of your youth. You may have forgotten them, God hasn't.

What is your most valuable possession? Isn't it your life? Your car, your eyes, your money, etc. adultery are all useless if you are dead. So obviously your life is the most precious thing you have. If you are in your right mind, you will want to live a happy life and live a long one; yet you have God's promise that if you don't honor you parents, you will have neither (Ephesians 6:1).

The Sixth is, "You shall not kill." But Jesus warned that if we get angry without cause, we are in danger of judgment. If we hate our brother, God calls us a murderer. We can violate the spirit of the Law by attitude and intent.

Maybe you have the blood of abortion on your hands. Civil law may smile upon your crime - God's Law calls you a murderer and the Sixth Commandment demands your death.

The Seventh is, "You shall not commit adultery." Who of us can say we are pure, when Jesus said that we violate this command in spirit, by lusting after a member of the opposite sex. He warned, "You have heard it said by them of old, "You shall not commit adultery," but I say to you, whoever looks upon a woman to lust after her, has committed adultery already with her in his heart." Until you find peace with God, you will be like a man who steals a T.V. set. He enjoys the programs, but deep within his heart is the knowledge that at any moment there could be a knock on the door, and the law could bring him to justice.

Remember that He has seen every sin you've ever committed. He has seen the deepest thoughts and desires of your heart. Nothing is hid from His pure eyes. The day will come when you have to face that Law you have broken. The Scriptures say that the impure (those who are not pure in heart), the immoral (fornicators - those who have sex before marriage) and adulterers will not enter the Kingdom of God. Adultery carries the death penalty.

The Eighth is "You shall not steal." Have you ever taken something that belonged to someone else? Then you are a thief. You cannot enter God's Kingdom.

You may have stolen a book from a library, failed to pay a parking fine, or maybe you "borrowed" something and never returned it. God is not impressed with the *value* of what you stole. When you have stolen, you have sinned against God, you have violated His Law.

The Ninth Commandment is, "You shall not bear false witness." Have you ever told a fib, a "white" lie, a half truth, and exaggeration? Then you have lied. How many lies do you have to tell to be a liar? Just one - "*All* liars will have their part in the Lake of Fire" (Scripture cannot be broken). You and I might not think that deceitfulness is a serious sin. God does.

The final nail in our coffin is, "You shall not covet." That means that we should not desire things that belong to others. Who of us can say we are innocent? All of us has sinned. As the Scriptures say, "There is none righteous, no, not one; There is none that understands, there is none that seeks after God." Just as with civil law, you don't have to break ten laws to be a law breaker, so the Bible warns, "Whosoever shall keep the whole Law, yet offend in one point, the same is guilty of all." The most blind of us will usually admit that man has glaring faults, we are forever transgressing against each other. But our transgressions are vertical, not horizontal; our real crimes are against God, not man. Without the Law, we look at sin from the standard of man; we have a distorted view. It takes the Law to give us insight to His standard, which is utter perfection. The Bible asks, "Who shall ascend the Hill of the Lord? - He that has clean hands and a pure heart;" "Blessed are the pure in heart, for they shall see God;" "Be perfect as your Father in Heaven is perfect." How do you measure up? Are you perfect, pure, holy, just and good? Or have you caught a glimpse of what you must look like to God? The picture the Scriptures paint of us is not a nice one.

This may sound strange, but the worst thing you can do at this point of time is to say that you will change your lifestyle. You will, from this day forward, live a good life. Let's say you were actually able to do that; from now on you will always not only *live* a good life, but *think* pure thoughts. Who then is going to forgive your past sins! Can a judge let a murderer go scott free because he promises to live a good life from now on? No, he's in debt to justice. He must be punished.

CHAPTER 17
THE REPELLENT

In the last chapter, with your permission, we "tapped the web" of your heart with the stick of God's Law. The reason for this was to see if we could make the ugly spider of your sinful nature reveal itself from his hiding. I trust that he has come out in the open; that for the first time you have seen what you are in the sight of a holy God - a guilty sinner. As the Scriptures say, "We are all as an unclean thing."

The truth is, you have violated the Law a multitude of times. The Law, like a dam of eternal justice, has been cracked in numerous places and is towering over your head waiting to burst upon you. The Bible says "the wrath of God" abides on you. Jesus warned that if the stone of a just and holy God falls on you, it will "grind you to powder." When you grind something to powder, you do a thorough job. Every foul skeleton in the closet of every human heart, will be bought out on the Day of Judgment.

The thought may have entered your mind that perhaps God will overlook your sins. Perhaps He, in His mercy, could just look the other way. If He does so, then He is unjust. Think of it again in connection with civil law. Can a judge look the other way when a criminal is obviously guilty, and be true to what is right? Even if the judge feels sorry for the criminal, he must stay true to the law, justice must be done. In the ten years between 1980 and 1990, in the United States alone, there were 60,000 murderers *who were never caught!* At least 60,000 murders were committed, and the murderers got away totally free. No doubt the figure is higher as many "accidents" and "suicides" are actually murders in disguise. These are people who have raped, tortured and strangled helpless victims; cutting up their bodies, or burning them without trace. Should God overlook their crimes on Judgment Day? Should He turn a blind eye? Should He compromise eternal justice? Or are you saying God should punish only the *serious* crimes? But your lying, stealing, adultery of the heart and rebellion *are* serious in His sight. No, the Bible says He will by no means clear the guilty. Who would like to see justice overlooked? Isn't it only the guilty?

Well, what is the punishment for sin? The Bible warns of everlasting damnation. It speaks of eternal Hell. Imagine if Hell was just a place of continual thirst. Have you ever had a thirst where you thought you'd die for lack of liquid? Or imagine if it were only a place of gnawing hunger? Or merely chronic toothache? Have you ever been in pain where you feel you want to die? Have you ever felt the pain of a broken arm, leg or rib? The Scriptures warn that Hell will be a place of "weeping and gnashing of teeth"; a place of eternal torment; a place where death will not bring welcome relief to suffering. A place where God will withdraw every blessing He has showered upon sinful, rebellious, ungrateful humanity. An abode where there will be absence of color, goodness, peace, beauty, love and laughter. A place of darkness, depression and despair, where murderers, rapists, those who have tortured, those who have stolen, lied, hated, been greedy, lustful, envious, jealous, blasphemous and rebellious to the command of God will dwell. Hell is the place where sinful humanity will receive its just retribution for crimes against the Law of a Holy God. *How terrible sin must be in the sight of God, to merit such just punishment!*

How's your conscience? Is it doing its duty? Is it accusing you of sin? Is it affirming the Commandments to be right? If not, which of the Commandments do you say is unjust - "You shall not steal," "You shall not bear false witness," "You shall not kill"? Perhaps you have committed adultery, or you have been longing for opportunity to. While no human being can point a accusing finger at you, the Ten Fingers of God's Holy Law stand as your accuser. You have been caught holding a smoking gun. The Law calls for your blood. Under it, the penalty for adultery is death by stoning. I don't stand as your accuser, I hang my head in guilt as one who has been in your place. I, like every other red-blooded male, was an adulterer at heart. I could not, in good conscience, call for justice to take its course.

CAUGHT IN THE ACT

You are like the woman caught in the very act of adultery. The Ten Great Rocks of the Law are waiting to beat down upon you. My earnest prayer is that you will not attempt to justify yourself at all, but bow your head and agree with the Law and the impartial voice of your conscience, and say, "Guilty!. . .what must I do?" In doing so, you are merely saying that God's testimony about humanity is true; that our hearts *are* deceitfully wicked, to a point of not only being vile sinners, but of being so deceitful that we will not even admit our own sins!

Like the woman, you have no other avenue to take. Your only hope is to fall at the feet of the Son of God. Ironically, there is only One human being who can call for justice to be done. And yet He is the only one who can forgive sins. At His feet alone, is the Law satisfied. If you humbly call on His name, you will hear, "Where are your accusers?" and be able to say, like the woman, "None Lord."

How could this be? Did God somehow compromise His justice through His Son. No! His justice was satisfied *through* His Son. What has happened is that the Law has stirred up the judge of conscience. The reason you could sin and not be concerned, was because the judge had been wooed into a deep slumber. The thunderings of the Law awoke him and now he stands as your accuser. There is an air of indignation that he has been silenced for so long. He has come back from his slumber with a vengeance, and with each Commandment he says, "Guilty!" What then must you do to satisfy his charges? No monetary payment will quieten his accusation of liability; no prison sentence will silence his righteous charge. What is it that will free you from the torments of what the world calls a "guilty conscience"? The Bible says that there is only one thing that can do it - the blood of Jesus Christ, ". . .How much more shall the blood of Christ, who through the eternal Spirit offered Himself without spot to God, *purge your conscience from dead works* to serve the Living God?" (italics added). In other words, anything you might try to do to save yourself from the consequences of sin, is nothing but "dead works."

Let's go back to civil law. Imagine you had broken the law. You are guilty of some terrible crime. You don't have two beans to rub together; *there's nothing you can do to redeem yourself.* Justice is about to take its course, when someone you don't even know steps into the courtroom and pays the fine for you! If that happened, the demands of the law are totally satisfied by the one who paid your fine. You are free to go from the courtroom. *That's what God did for you and I.* When the Law utterly condemned us, Jesus Christ stepped into the courtroom and paid the fine for us by His own precious blood.

Words fail me to express His love which was demonstrated to us on that cross so long ago. When the Law called for our blood, Jesus gave His. When the justice of a holy God cried out for retribution, Jesus cried out on the cross in agony as He satisfied it, by giving Himself on our behalf. The Law didn't just demand the death of the Son of God, it demanded the *suffering death of the perfect sinless Messiah.* Sin is such a serious thing in the sight of God, the only thing that would satisfy His righteousness was the unspeakable suffering of a sinless sacrifice.

I heard the story of an African chief who got wind of a mutiny being planned in his tribe. In an effort to quash the revolt, he called the tribe together, and said that anyone caught in rebellion would be given one hundred lashes, *without mercy.* A short time later, to the chief's dismay, he found that his own brother was at the bottom of the revolt. He was trying to overthrow him so that he could be head of the tribe. Everyone thought the chief would break his word. But being a just man, he had his brother tied to a tree. Then he had himself tied next to him, *and he took those 100 lashes across his own bare flesh.* In doing so, he not only kept his word; justice was done, *but he also demonstrated his great love and forgiveness towards his brother.*

When God became flesh in the Messiah and suffered on the cross, He was not only showing that God was just, but He was also demonstrating the depth of His love and forgiveness towards you and I. Can you imagine how that brother felt as the chief took the punishment which was due to him? Can't you see how every lash of the whip would break his own rebellious heart. Can't you see tears well in his eyes, and his face wince as he heard each lash of the whip? Is your own heart so hard that you can hear the nails being driven into the pure hands of the Son of God, and not at all be moved by such love? Isn't there a cry in your own heart, as you hear the agonies of the cross, as the fury of a holy, just and righteous God was unleashed against Him. . .or have you a heart of stone? He suffered in our place, taking *our* punishment; may God make it real to you.

Let's go back to the plane analogy for a moment. Imagine if I had spent a great deal of effort in trying to persuade you to put your parachute on, by talking to you about the horrible consequences of breaking the law of gravity. I had been "hanging you out the plane by your ankles," speaking of what would happen to you if you hit the ground at 120 mph. Your eyes widened as I went into dctails. But, slowly it dawned on you that if you wanted to live, you had better put the parachute on. Suddenly, you are convinced. It needs no more words from me. With trembling hand, you reach under your seat, *to find to your horror that there is no parachute!* Terror *really* gets a grip on you now, as you think of the horrific death you have to face at any moment. As you sit there in a daze, you are awakened from your living nightmare by a kindly voice. Another passenger you have never seen before, is holding a parachute out for you to take. You reach out and take it in your trembling hands. Words can't express your gratitude. An unspeakable joy fills your heart, as you realize that you don't have to die. The thought as to where the stranger got the parachute from hardly enters your mind.

After the jump, you find that all the other passengers have lived. . . *all but one.* It's only then you realize that the stranger gave you his own parachute, *and went to his death so that you could live.*

That is what Jesus Christ did for you. He gave His life that you might be saved. A complete Stranger, Someone you didn't even know, did that for you. His was a willing, terrible, substitutionary death.

WHAT SHOULD YOU THEN DO?

What you must do, is for the first time in your life, truly obey the command of God to repent and put your trust totally and singularly in Jesus Christ. Your alternative is to have the full fury of God's Law unleashed against you on Judgment Day. You have no other option - *unless you repent, you shall perish.* There is no purgatory, no second chance, no other name, no other hope, no other way for you to be saved. Pray a prayer like this from your heart: "Dear God, I have violated your Law. I have broken your Commandments. I have sinned against You and You only. You have seen every thought and deed. You saw the sins of my youth, and the unclean desires of my heart. I am truly sorry. I now understand how serious my transgressions have been. If justice was to be done, and all my sins uncovered on the Day of Judgment, I know I would be guilty, and justly end up in Hell. Words cannot express my gratitude for the substitutionary death of the Lord Jesus Christ. I may not have a tear in my eye, but there is one in my heart. I *really* am sorry. From this day forward, I will show my gratitude for your mercy by living a life that is pleasing in your sight. I will read your Word daily and obey what I read. In Jesus' name I pray, Amen."

CHAPTER 18
A HOPEFUL PRESUMPTION

I am going to make a hopeful presumption. I am trusting that you have made a committal of your life to Jesus Christ, so now I want to share some very important thoughts with you in the following chapters. If you are already a Christian, please read on, because what I am going to say concerns you also. If you have made a commitment, God will prove Himself faithful to you, as He has to me and millions of others down through the ages. All that is required of you is your obedience. Read the Bible *daily*. Believe His promises, remembering that there is no greater insult to God than not to believe His promises.

HANG IN THERE
There was once a daring escape from a Nazi war prison. The inmates had dug a tunnel, which sadly had surfaced twenty feet short of the cover of a wooded area. So they waited until a moonless night, and sent one man into the woods to watch for when the guard turned his back. His job was to pull on a piece of string which ran from the woods down into the tunnel. This let the next prisoner know that it was safe for him to emerge. One by one the men felt the tug of the string and surfaced, running into

131

the safety of the dark woods. Unfortunately the guard heard a sound, and walked across to the area where the hole was. He didn't see the opening, but stood by it for some time, looking suspiciously around the locality. Time seemed to stand still for the next prisoner, who was waiting underground for the tug on the string.

Suddenly, he lost patience. He could stand it no longer. He moved forward, then up out of the hole in the dark. It was the last thing he did. The guard swung around and fired on him with his machine gun, filling him full of lead.

We can learn from that man's fatal mistake. His error was three-fold. He lacked patience, faith and obedience. If only he had trusted the one on the other end. If only he had obeyed instructions given to him, he would have found his freedom; *but instead, he lost his very life.*

The Bible tells us that we inherit the promises of God through "faith and patience." There will be times in your Christian walk when you will ask God for something, and there will be a delay. Don't lose patience, hang in there. The One holding onto the string can see things you can't, He knows what is best for you. Obey His Instruction Book and trust in the Lord with "all your heart, and don't lean to your own understanding." Don't trust your judgments, or your emotions. If you have obeyed the Gospel, you are now in a different Kingdom - God does things totally different to the way you are used to. Becoming a Christian is like leaving your country and moving to another. There are radical culture shocks. In 1989, my wife and I and our three kids moved 8,000 miles from New Zealand to the United States. Although our country is similar to the U.S., we did find that there was a slight "culture shock." Downunder, we drive on the other side of the road. The change from "left means life, right means death" to the opposite is simple - until you come to an intersection and have to make a left turn. Only once, in the first week, did I drive on the wrong side of the road. Sue gently screamed, which told me something was wrong.

Also, the Downunder cars have the steering wheel on the other side of the car. After coming out of a supermarket I opened the door, sat in my vehicle and wondered who on earth would want to steal my steering wheel! I felt more foolish than anything. My pride had been hurt. I made out I was playing around in the glove compartment until I saw that no one had seen my little error.

PANE IN THE NOSE

Pride is a subtle thing. I remember many years ago, stepping forward to take a closer look at a sofa in a shop display. Suddenly I came to an abrupt halt. I had walked straight into a plate glass door. Did I give thought to the pain coming from a flattened nose? No. My first thought was, *"Who saw me!"* When I realized that no one had seen, I gave comfort to my nose.

I once saw a woman walk behind me while I was preaching outdoors. As she did so, she stumbled and twisted her ankle. Didn't hurt at all. With the utmost composure, she graciously walked across in front of the crowd as though nothing had happened. Yet from my viewpoint, I saw that when she got around the corner, she doubled up with pain.

The Bible says God hates pride. It is a sin that will stop multitudes from entering the Kingdom of Heaven. Pride destroys families. It stops a husband or wife from admitting wrong. They would rather break up a family and keep their pride, than humble themselves and be reconciled, even for the sake of the children.

There were more blows to my pride. Other adjustments in our move to the U.S. were relatively minor. Downunder light switches are "up" for off, and "down" for on. The water goes down the drain the opposite way, and a check means "correct," with a cross meaning "wrong." Also, Downunder, a "fag" is a cigarette butt, not a homosexual. This last colloquialism is minor until one uses the word while preaching. I was preaching outdoors in Hawaii, when a drunken heckler began yelling at me. He called himself a Christian, even though he was drunk and had a cigarette hanging from his mouth. After a bit of an exchange, much to my consternation, he began to leave so I called, *"Going off for another fag huh?"* The crowd roared, and I was left bewildered. Afterwards, I was filled in as to why I had that response. Anything else I should know?

My only other incident of like nature happened when I was asked to give blood at the local Red Cross. When we arrived, I spend quite some time filling out a form about my background. The aids virus left blood banks in justified paranoia. Ordinary banks are worried about bad withdrawals; blood banks, bad deposits. The list seemed endless. Had I had aids, did I have heart disease, did I have fainting spells? etc. I looked down the list then across to the boxes on the right side of the form. Simple. All they contained were **"Yes," "No."** So I went down the boxes and did what all good Downunders do, I crossed out the non-applicable one. Had I aids? Crossed out the "Yes," leaving a clear "No" for the person marking the form. Made sense to me. I then took the form to the nurse and sat beside her. She stared at it for about three seconds, then looked at me in horror. The form said that I had aids, hepatitis, typhoid, malaria, cancer, heart disease, lumps under my arms, skin rashes, fainting spells and that I'd had diarrhea for over a month among other things! Her facial expression changed when I told her that New Zealanders walk around up-side-down, drive on the other side of the road, and fill out forms differently.

So, in one sense, you have in your commitment to Christ, moved into a different culture. You are now living in a Kingdom which has rules that are radical compared to what you have been used to. You have bowed the knee to the sovereignty of the King of Kings, now you owe your allegiance to Him, above all else. . .and His ways *are* different. Never a man spoke like this man. Jesus said to "love your enemies," "turn the other cheek," to "do good to those who despitefully use you." Many have missed the point of why the Christian should let another person stomp on top of him. The reason is not that the Christian is a wimp, but that he has committed the job of vengeance to the Lord. If someone does me wrong, I am not to take the law into my own hands; no, I give it all to God in prayer, and if, in His perfect judgment, He sees fit to do so, He will stomp on the person what stomped on me...and He has a righteous (and bigger) stomp.

Let me give you some examples of how it works. Sue and I used to let ones take our books and tapes on a credit system. After a seminar, if someone didn't have any money at that time, we let them take what they wanted, and we sent them a bill. It was a good system, except for the fact, that after some time we found that we had $3,000 worth of unpaid bills. Professing Christians were taking our property and not paying for them. We sent reminders. That didn't produce any response at all. So we decided we would get radical and do it God's way. We mailed each of those who had stolen books and tapes from us, a gift of $10, based on the fact that Jesus said to do good to those that despitefully use you. He said that if someone took your coat, give them your cloak also. What we were saying was, "God we give it all to you, we want you to be our financial adviser. If you see fit to stomp on these people, that's up to you. You know their circumstances, perhaps they are in financial difficulty. In the meantime, we will love our neighbors as ourselves and do them good." The following weekend, I did a series of meetings for a church, and found that the honorarium they gave me *was ten times the normal amount!* We like the way God works, so we now do things His way.

This wasn't just an isolated incident. I once sent 14 boxes of books to South Africa. When they arrived, the person who ordered them called me and said that they were all damaged. We were 4,000 miles apart, so all I could do was to ask him to claim the insurance. For some reason, he refused. A friend told me to instigate court proceedings, but I felt to draw on the wisdom of my Business Adviser; so I gave the whole thing to God in prayer and wrote it off. The next weekend at one Christian camp, *we sold over seven times as many books and tapes as we usually sell!*

A close friend of mine is a partner in a Christian T-shirt company. One of their shirts had a particular word on it that was used by a well-known apparel company. Soon after the shirt was released, my friend was informed by the company that they would take them to court for using the word, if they didn't come up with a quick $10,000. Even though he was told by his lawyers there was no way they could lose the case in court, he prayed about it and felt to obey the Scriptures. Jesus said if someone sues you for your coat, *give them your cloak also*, so he gave them a number of checks (over a short period of time) totaling $10,000, then another one for $1,000. He sent the checks to the apparel company stating the Biblical reason for each of the checks. What he did didn't make much sense.

Within one month, God had so blessed the T-shirt company, they moved from eight employees to forty two. In fact, within three years of business, *they have sold over one million T-shirts!*

You may not be involved in book or T-shirt sales, but you can put these same principles into practice. If someone does you wrong, stop for a minute and say, "What would man have me do? And what would Jesus have me do?" Man's way is to "stick up for your rights". . .and that will be a way that feels good to your natural mind, a way that seems right; but give it all to God in prayer, then do it *His* way.

If someone wrongs you at your place of work, buy him a gift. Do him good, then pray that through God's love, you might touch his heart and open him up to listen to the claims of the Gospel.

CHAPTER 19
WATCH AND PRAY

While I was preaching outdoors once, someone once called out, "If you were a Christian, you would give me your watch!" So without being distracted from what I was saying I slipped off the watch and handed it to him. I forgot that the watch had "American revival - pray without ceasing" across its face. When he saw it, I was told later that he made the "sign of a cross"!? and gave it to someone else to give back to me. I wonder what upset him? Was it the word "pray," or perhaps "revival?" Most non-Christians don't know what the word revival means. It has even lost its sense in many contemporary Christian circles. To many it means no more than a sweating, loose-tied preacher, stirring up a congregation for two or three nights; much singing, many decisions, then everyone goes home, and all is forgotten in a few weeks. True revival is a sovereign move of God, such as happened in Wales at the turn of the century. So many were converted, the police were out of work. Bars were empty. Even the coal miner's mules had to be retrained because their owners were no longer cursing and speaking harshly to them. Now they were gentle, loving masters, and the mules didn't recognize the commands!

Once I was meditating while in the shower on all the problems besetting the United States - the millions of abortions, the murders, the violence, the family breakdowns, wife beatings, child molestations, rape, the greed, the diseases flooding the nation, the sky-rocketing suicide rates, the floods, earthquakes, the loneliness, the fear, the suffering, pain, and the fear of death tormenting humanity. Then I thought about the terror of Judgment Day and the inevitability of Hell for those who reject God's mercy. My mind seemed to reel in confusion as to what I should do as a Christian. Suddenly I looked up at the shower unit. It was one of those pulsating types with the instructions around the outside. These instructions were different though. Somehow they had become caught up when the unit turned, leaving nothing but a jumbled mess. There were e's and a's, y's and p's. Nothing made sense; it was just a mass of disarray, that is except for one word. The "s" had been scraped off the word spray, leaving alone among the confusion the word, **"pray."**

As Christians, that is what you and I can do to help the United States. We all can pray. Charles Finney said, "What constitutes a spirit of prayer? Is it many prayers and warm words? No, it is a state of continual desire and anxiety of mind, for the salvation of sinners." That should be the basic attitude of mind within every Christian. But what is it that we should be requesting of God? There are the daily necessities of life, our "daily bread" etc, but Jesus told us specifically to pray for "laborers." I can't find anywhere is Scripture where we are told to pray for sinners, but we are told to pray for laborers. That's what is needed to bring revival to America. A laborer is one who is prepared to go out into the harvest fields and sweat for the Kingdom of God. While there are thousands in the U.S.

who *are* laboring for God, many have been left without the needed "sickle" - because of ignorance, they are trying to reap with their bare hands.

You may be familiar with the "soap bubble" message of the modern gospel. It is one that promises love, joy, peace and fulfillment to those who give their lives to Christ; when the promise of Scripture for those who follow Jesus, is tribulation, temptation, persecution and everlasting life. The last one is the frosting on the cake, making the first three almost bearable.

One thing I feel I am called to do (with the help of God), is to burst the soap bubble, then encourage the Church back from the modern gospel to the Biblical presentation of the way of salvation. Instead of telling sinners that Jesus will make them happy, we must warn them that God's wrath is abiding on them and that they need to repent. The correct way to do this is to use the Law of God to bring the knowledge of sin. I have endeavored to do this in this publication, so go over the different chapters and become familiar with the way this is done. The reason you need to do this is because, if you are going to be a laborer, you will want to be effective.

It is vital that you do have a concern for the lost, not only for their sake, but for yours. Love for your neighbor's eternal welfare is one sign that you have been converted. You will have a new heart with new desires. You will naturally love God, and you will also naturally love your neighbor. This is because the New Covenant promise was that God would put His Law into our hearts, causing us to

141

do the things that please Him, by nature. While in an unconverted state, it was "natural" to walk in rebellion to His will, now, because of the new birth, it is naturally our delight to want to fulfill His desires. This means that you will, as you see the plight of the lost, want to share with them the way of salvation. *You are desperately needed.* America is in trouble. Even the secular world knows that. Drug-lords, like devouring beasts are tearing at her fleshly boarders. She is bleeding from without, and broken and bruised from within.

Her youth, the very life of the nation are being destroyed by sin and shame. Thirty-three thousand get some sort of sexually transmitted disease *each day,* with 1.2 *million* becoming pregnant each year! Despite the easy access to the temporal pleasures of free sex, literally thousands each year are mystifying experts, by choosing the escape of suicide.

Corruption among morally-blind political leaders can only take the U.S. into the "ditch" Jesus warned both leaders and followers would fall. The unthinkable is happening - families are more than disintegrating - fathers are murdering their children; husbands, their wives. Despite *T.V. Guide*'s recent poll revealing that 96 percent of Americans believe in God, rape, racial violence, murder, theft, gambling, adultery and abortion are on the rampage. Pornographic video producers can hardly feed the demand. Twenty million pornographic magazines are sold *each week!* The most popular movies carry warnings that they need parental guidance; in other words they contain, perversions, sex, blasphemy and violence. In fact the average 16 year old American has seen 200,000 acts of violence and 32,000 murders. Homosexuality is now seen as an acceptable alternative lifestyle, with 100,000 "gays" living in San Francisco and an estimated 17,000,000 nation-wide. The plague of aids has not only taken tens of thousands of homosexuals to a humiliating and agonizing death, it is now reaching into the heterosexual community. In the late seventies, godless judges opened the floodgates of the murderous spirit of abortion, which, *in one decade,* has taken the lives of over 10,000,000 Americans.

Despite her belief in God, it is estimated that 140,000,000 shoplifting offenses occur each year. In 1987 13,000,000 video recorders were stolen, every 78 seconds someone is robbed, every five minutes someone is raped, every 33 seconds a car is stolen and every 10 seconds, a burglar strikes. *Over 40,000,000 Americans are the victims of violent crime each year!* So many people are packed into U.S. prisons, judges are being forced to release guilty criminals back onto the street *without even bringing prosecution.*

Throughout the nation, sad and pathetic photos of her kidnapped beloved children are displayed in the hope that they will be returned before they are sexually abused or used in some horrific satanic ritual. School children are gunned down while at school, or molested in the classroom or at home. Anti-semitism, Naziism and racial hatred boil beneath the surface of the nation, waiting to explode. Literally thousands roam the streets, victims of society, alcohol or drugs. Millions are trapped by fear - fear of their fellow man, fear of the future, fear of cancer, fear of the all too common earthquakes, droughts, tornadoes and floods.

UNCOVERED SKIRTS

Meanwhile, despite her 1485 Christian radio stations and over 300 Christian television stations, the "salt of the earth" is being trampled under foot. In 1988, a leading Christian Magazine conducted a confidential survey among 300 pastors. In the survey, 23 percent admitted that they had been involved in some sort of sexual immorality. *That's one in five pastors!* If that's the state of the shepherds, what must the flocks be like? The news media take delight in uncovering the skirts of the Church, with regular prime-time television devoted to her many glaring scandals.

The problem is that the Church has forsaken the true message of salvation, that the way into the Kingdom of God is a "straight gate" and a "narrow way." We have made the issue to be "happiness," rather than one of "righteousness" then with manipulative music and appeals to the emotions rather than the will and conscience, we have opened wide our doors to the world and its sins. We have sown our own seed, that the way of entry is broad and easy, and reaped a "mixed multitude," evidenced by the state of the contemporary Church.

Now from within the Army of God come many uncertain sounds. There are trumpet calls from "peace and safety," to gloom and judgment, and the irony is that both extremes are coming from spiritually respected sources. Some are saying that America's sexual sins are worse than that of Sodom and Gomorrah, or that she is beyond redemption. Others carry on with a positive confession of prosperity as though all were well.

A FREE FACIAL

A number of years ago, at some expense I ran a series of advertisements on television, in which I attempted to warn parents about occultic music which advocated murder. After the adverts were screened I wondered if I would get my face re-arranged. I remember sitting in my parked car a week after they were screened, transfixed as a gentleman, with clenched fist and a determined look, walked up to my car and grim-faced, asked, "Are you Ray Comfort?" After I said I was, *he then thrust his hand through the opened window, dropped $20 in my lap and walked off*. . .much to my relief! I guess it was his way of saying "Thanks."

It would seem that God delights in bringing victory out of disastrous situations. As Israel stood helplessly by the Red Sea, trapped by their enemies with no possible way of escape, God did the impossible. With Daniel, God brought victory out of disaster. With Lazarus He did the impossible. What great horror, darkness, hopelessness and death surrounded Golgotha, yet from it came the ultimate, glorious victory of the resurrection. To say that America is in a dark, hopeless state is the understatement of the century. Satan holds America in his cold, clenched, iron fist, in resolute rebellion. His work is blatantly evident - disease, crime, fear, violence, greed, murder, rape, pornography, suicide, adultery, alcoholism, drug-addiction, racism, the occult, marriage breakdown just to name a few. Add to this God's anger against sin, and the whole situation looks utterly disastrous for this great but sinking nation. Yet God, in His sovereignty can, in a moment of time open Satan's iron grip and drop the riches of revival in the lap of the Church, "where sin abounds, there much more does grace abound." Let the Church prepare herself for that revival. Let us believe that God will extend the same merciful hand of deliverance to this sinful and adulterous generation, as He extended to you and I. Meanwhile, we must obey the Divine commandment to "lift up our voice like a trumpet" and show this people their transgression. If this generation doesn't see that it has offended a *holy* God, a God of justice, truth and righteousness, it will not repent. Those who see God in truth do not carry on in sin. Let us work in with the Holy Spirit, and allow Him to pray through us with "groanings that cannot be uttered" in travailing prayer, that God might bring to birth His purposes in the closing hours of time. Let's forget our past failings, and through faith look *beyond* the Red Sea, look *past* the lions' mouths, turn from Lazarus' tomb *to* the Son of God, and look to Him to give us our heart's desire. . .for with God *nothing* shall be impossible.

CHAPTER 20
SATAN'S STRATEGY

In the earlier chapters I have stated of the necessity to use the Law in evangelism? Is this Biblical? To answer the question let's look to the Scriptures.

A GOOD REASON
One very good reason why we should use the Law to evangelize, is because Jesus did. In Luke 10:25, when a professing expert in God's Law asked how he could inherit eternal life, Jesus didn't give him the good news of the cross, He pointed him to the Law of God. This man was proud and impenitent, so Jesus used the Law to bring "the knowledge of sin." Similarly in Luke 18:18, when another asked how he could inherit eternal life, Jesus didn't give him grace, He gave him the Law to show him his error. This man had broken the first of the Ten Commandments by making mammon his God. The Law brought light to his darkened understanding; that's its function, "The Commandment is a lamp and the Law is light" (Proverbs 6:23).

If you read Matthew 15 in conjunction with Mark 7, you will see that Jesus used the Law to bring the knowledge of sin to godless Pharisees, specifically using the 1st, 3rd, 5th, 6th, 7th, 8th, 9th and the 10th Commandments. In Mark 12:29, when a scribe had a right understanding of the Law, Jesus said, "You are not far from the Kingdom of God;" in other words the Law was acting as a "schoolmaster" to give him understanding and lead him to grace. He used the 7th commandment for the same purpose when dealing with the adulterous woman at the well, in John Chapter four, and He taught the multitudes using the Law many times in the Sermon on the Mount. Jesus not only used the Law to instruct sinners, but He commended those who do so by saying they would be "great" in the Kingdom of God (Matthew 5:19).

MERCY FOR THE PENITENT
However, when ones approached the Son of God in humility and contrition, Jesus gave them grace, as in the case of Nicodemus, Nathaniel and others. Remember the woman caught in the very act of breaking the 7th Commandment. The wrath of the Law put her between a rock and a hard place, driving her to the mercy of God in Christ. Those who have faced the wrath of God's justice, thoroughly embrace the grace of God, and go their way and sin no more. Grace being given to the humble is seen in other portions of scripture. When the Gospel (the good news of God's grace) was preached, it was either to Jews, who knew the Law (and therefore had a sense of sin), or to those who "feared God and worked righteousness." But when the Gospel was preached to the *ungodly,* it was always proceeded by the Law of God to bring the knowledge of sin, for a man will not repent if he doesn't know what sin is.

The Apostle Paul used the Law when dealing with the ungodly, as seen in his preaching at Athens. These were Gentiles who had no understanding of sin (Acts 17:30), so Paul used the first and the second of the Ten Commandments to show them that they were idolaters, that they had sinned against God and therefore needed to repent. When dealing with hard-hearted Jews in Acts 28:23, he also used "the Law of Moses." Paul tells us why he did so. Its function is to "stop the mouth" i.e. to stop sinners justifying themselves, leaving the whole world guilty before God (Romans 3:19). In Romans 3:20 he tells us that the Law brings "the knowledge of sin," *in fact he said that he didn't even know what sin was until the Law told him* (Romans 7:7).

If Paul needed the Law to show him God's standard of righteousness, how much more does this lawless generation! Why do they have no regard for the commandments of God, with their adultery, lying, theft, murder and covetousness? - because "without the Law, the sense of (sin) is inactive" (Romans 7:8 Amplified Bible). The very purpose of the Law is to act as a "schoolmaster to bring us to Christ" (Galatians 3:24), to show sin in its true light, that it is "exceedingly sinful" (Romans 7:13).

FOR WHAT WAS IT DESIGNED?
The Law's function is so clearly seen in 1 Timothy 1:8, "The Law is good, if anyone uses it lawfully, for the purpose for which it was designed" (Ampl. Bible). Well, what was the Law "designed" for? The following verse tells us, "The Law was not made for a righteous man. . .but for sinners." This same portion of scripture tells us that the

Law was also designed to reach homosexuals (1 Timothy 1:10).

If we desire to see Israel saved, we must preach the Law to them. They are in the dilemma they are in *because they have forsaken the Law of their God.* If we take the Law to them, it will act as a schoolmaster to bring them to Christ. God tells us in scripture that His people are "destroyed through lack of knowledge." What is there a lack of knowledge of?   His Law (Hosea 4:6). If they have no knowledge of the Law, they won't know what sin is, and if they don't know what sin is, they won't repent; and if they won't repent, they will perish (Luke 13:3). The Law will show Israel the holiness of God and drive them to grace, as it did in Acts Chapter 2.

If we want to reach the Moslem world, we must take advantage of the fact that they accept Moses as a prophet. When we preach "Moses" (the Law) to them, they will see the futility of their own self righteous efforts, and thus be driven to the only One who can make them clean in the sight of a Holy Creator. If they will not hear Moses, neither will they be persuaded though one rose from the dead. The Law gives reason for the cross.

MORE GOOD REASONS
James not only used the Law to bring the knowledge of sin (James 2: 7-10), he gave it honor by referring to it as the "royal" Law and the "perfect Law of liberty." He spoke of sinners being "convinced of the Law as transgressors."

I have heard it said that Peter was a better preacher than

Paul because of the fact that 3,000 souls responded to his preaching. To whom was Peter speaking? - godly Jews, "devout" Jews, who therefore ate, drank and slept God's Law! So when Peter preached, he didn't give them Law; no, they already had the knowledge of sin; he just told them the good news of Christ redeeming them from the curse of the Law, they were "pricked in the heart," and cried out to be saved. The Law was a schoolmaster to bring them to Christ.

John the Baptist also preached the Law when he reproved Herod of his adultery (Mark 6:18), saying that it was not "lawful" to have his brother's wife. However, the thrust of John's message was to Israel, *to those who knew the Law*. So as soon as John said "Come and acknowledge your sins," multitudes flocked to him for a baptism of repentance (Luke 16:16). The Law made them "press into" the Kingdom of God. It made them "hunger and thirst for righteousness." Like a drowning man who suddenly sees his plight, they became violent, and took hold of the Kingdom of God by force. This is clearly stated in Matthew 11: 12 & 13.

THESE MEN BEING DEAD YET SPEAK

The Law was the essence of the Gospel proclamation of John Wesley, Charles Finney, D.L. Moody, Whitefield and Charles Spurgeon. Their evangelical efforts were zeal *with* knowledge because they knew the secret to revival. In fact, they warned that if the church failed to use the Law, it would do nothing but fill the Church with false converts.

In Luke 11:52, Jesus strongly rebuked the lawyers (those

who should have been teaching God's Law), saying, "Woe unto you lawyers, for you have taken away the key of knowledge. . ." That key of knowledge is the Law of God. It unlocks the Door of the Savior; it is the schoolmaster to bring us to Christ. Let's not dishonor the Law by failing to use it for the purpose for which it was given. God says that it is perfect, holy, just and good, promising that He would "magnify the Law and make it honorable." It is the very "form of knowledge and truth" (Romans 2:20).

When we get a grip of its purpose, to bring souls into the Kingdom, we will say with the Psalmist, "Oh how I love your Law, it is my meditation all the day." We will say with the Apostle of Grace "I delight in the Law of God." When we use the Law in evangelism, we will work in with the Holy Spirit who convicts the world of sin (which is transgression *of* the Law (1 John 3:4)), righteousness (which is *of* the Law) and judgment (which is *by* the Law (Romans 2:12)). The "work of the Law" which is in the heart of every man (Romans 2:15) will then affirm the truth of each Commandment, giving the knowledge of sin and showing need of the Savior. This is not a debate over Calvinism or Armenianism. What I'm saying is that we need to preach the way God instructs us to, and leave the results up to Him.

EQUIPPING THE SAINTS
To equip the soldiers of Christ with the weapon of the Law will be to replace a one shot "muzzle loader" with a gattling gun, putting new found courage in the heart. No longer will the enemy advance with such strength, because the Army of God will be fit for the battle. Even in the

SATAN'S STRATEGY

midst of spiritual warfare, they will have "great peace" because "they love your Law, and nothing will cause them to stumble" (Psalm 119:165).

Perhaps the most respected Bible Commentator of all time, would be Matthew Henry. Listen to what he had to say about the use of the Law: "As that which is straight discovers that which is crocked, as the looking-glass shows us our natural face with all its spots and deformities, *so there is no way of coming to that knowledge of sin which is necessary to repentance, and consequently to peace and pardon, but by comparing our hearts and lives with the Law,* . . .those that would know sin, *must get the knowledge of the Law in its strictness, extent, and spiritual nature. "*

I can think of no stronger way of putting the following fact. If we continue to evangelize, without the use of the Law to bring the knowledge of sin, *we will find that we are working for the devil, rather than for God.*

For every 1,000 decisions we get, we will create as many as 900 backsliders; and for the hundred who remain in the Church, at least 70 will become lukewarm in the areas of prayer, holiness, evangelism and having a hunger for the Word of God. Such "evangelism" is against the purposes of God, and a furtherance to the work of satan.

We can no longer afford to be ignorant of his devices. *Satan's strategy has been to blind the Church to this weapon of warfare, which is mighty through God to the pulling down of strongholds.*

On the other hand, those who pray "Open my eyes Lord that I might behold wondrous things out of your Law," will see the power of the Law to convert the soul. Those who come to Jesus Christ will be more than "decisions for Jesus"; they will be sinners who are *soundly* saved. They will be soul-winners, not pew-warmers, laborers, not layabouts, assets, not liabilities for the local church. Revival will then become a reality, and this world will be reached for Jesus Christ.

CHAPTER 21
THAT'S THE WAY

I recently attended an open board meeting at Hosanna Chapel (our home church), and found that we were being supported as "missionaries." I found this interesting because when people asked what I did at the Church, an "associate Pastor" didn't seem to fit, as I didn't do the normal duties of a pastor. For the first time I saw myself as a missionary from New Zealand to the Church in the United States. That seems to be the way God does things - He takes the nobodies from the uttermost part of the earth and brings them to a great nation like the U.S. to fulfill His purposes.

I had been meditating on this thought the week before I flew to Sacramento for a series of meetings. While I was waiting to speak there at a seminar, the Pastor stood up and said, "Ray Comfort is a missionary from New Zealand to the Church in the U.S." At that very instant, radio interference in the form of a voice abruptly broke into the sound system and said, "That's the way we do it...!" I had to agree.

During the same trip, I was scheduled to do a television interview. I prefer the interviewer to have read my book *Hell's Best Kept Secret*, so that he knows where I'm coming from, as most of the Church have never heard of the use of the Law in evangelism.

This day I was surprised to see that I had two interviewers and neither of them had read the book! So I took a deep breath and started at square one, about the Law of the Lord being perfect, converting the soul. Then I shared many Scriptures about the correct function of the Law. The guest interviewer (an ominous looking, well-dressed Pastor) held his peace for about 5 minutes, then jumped on me with, *"You mean to say you would beat him with the Law and leave him!"* I said, "If he was unrepentant, I would." If a sinner continues to blaspheme, curse and mock the things of God, I deliberately don't give him grace. As far as I am concerned (and I am open to correction), it is the casting of the ultimate pearl before swine. I leave the weight of the Law on his shoulders.

Why was the Pastor offended in the first place? It was because most in modern evangelism (perhaps unconsciously) demean the work of God in drawing sinners to Christ. They neglect to allow the Holy Spirit room to convict the sinner of sin, of righteousness and of judgment. As far as they are concerned, all the sinner has to do to be saved is to ask Jesus into his heart, while the Biblical truth is, "no man comes to the Son unless the Father draws him;" it is God that "gives repentance to the acknowledging of the truth." The bottom line is, if the Holy Spirit is not drawing a sinner I am witnessing to, I am wasting my time to press for any commitment. Those who don't care to trust God when seeking the lost, but rather prefer to do the job themselves will probably end up doing so. . .that is doing it without the help of God, and reaping false converts.

If evangelism is merely a matter of trying to convince someone to "give his heart to Jesus," then we don't need the Law or the help of God. But if we want to see someone born of God, to be saved from the wrath to come, then we need the Law as the instrument of God, to bring the knowledge of sin. That takes a lot of weight off our shoulders. God saves sinners, not us. We just plant good seed - He brings the increase. R.A. Torrey said, ". . .it is the Holy Spirit, not ourselves, who convicts men of sin. He does it through the truth we present, but we must realize our dependence upon Him and look to Him and count on Him to do the work." Therefore if I leave the weight of the Law on a hard heart, God will follow Him, convict him if He so sees fit, and bring him to a knowledge of grace at just the right time. If I do my part, God will be faithful and do His. We are co-laborers with God - the Spirit and the Bride say "Come." Jesus didn't run after the rich young ruler, trying to console him. No, the man loved his money more than he loved God. He was an impenitent transgressor of the First and the Tenth Commandment. After speaking of preaching the Law and judgment to come to a sinner, Augustine said, "He which hears, if he is not terrified, if he is not troubled, is not to be comforted." The Biblical way to witness is (with the help of God), to "break the hard heart, and heal the broken one" - Law to the proud, grace to the humble.

And what is the motive for doing such a thing? Is it because I like seeing people tormented by the Law? No, I want to see them saved from the fircs of an everlasting Hell. I don't want them to have a false conversion and end up in a worse state than before they heard the Gospel. A "decision for Jesus" is not enough, they must repent, and without the knowledge of sin which comes only by the Law, they cannot. Look at this quote from a booklet called *Decisional Regeneration* By J.E. Adams, "Jack Hyles, considered by many to be an authority on preaching, gives the following advice to his fellow-ministers: "Many of us in our preaching will make such statements as, "Now, in conclusion"; "Finally, may I say",; "My last point is. . ." These statements are sometimes dangerous. The sinner knows five minutes before you finish; hence he digs in and prepares himself for the invitation so that he does not respond. However, if your closing is abrupt and a lost person does not suspect that you are about finished, you have crept up on him and he will not have time to prepare himself for the invitation. Many people may be reached, using this method."

Then Mr. Adams comments in his booklet, "At the first reading of such a teaching one might believe, or at least hope, that he misread Mr. Hyles. The second, third and fourth readings, however, confirm that Mr. Hyles actually teaches that men may be converted to Christ as a result of some clever method a minister uses in his sermon, and that one's eternal destiny may be determined by the impulse of an unguarded moment. This idea that a man's salvation may depend upon his being "crept up on" and giving his unwilling consent is in direct conflict with what

Scriptures teach concerning the receiving of Jesus Christ."

Modern evangelical methods remind me of the Californian police sting operation I mentioned earlier. It subtly lures the sinner through the door of decision, trying to trap the unwilling victim into the Kingdom of God. Sue once spoke to a sailor who had been trapped by the propaganda of advertisements which painted the Navy as being a wonderful life, filled with challenge and excitement. After he joined, he found that it was nothing but hard work, and couldn't wait to leave. In this case, it would have been better for the Navy to have been honest in the first place, so that if he had signed up knowing what he was in for, at least he would be committed to the cause. The Christian navy has a mass of "recruits" who are ready to leave the first time they strike hard work.

The confusion in the hearts of sincere Christians comes because they do see some sinners soundly saved under such unbiblical methods. Adams answers this with, "It is true that some are converted under such preaching, but this is in spite of the false methods used, not because of them." The casualty rates from these methods are massive. If you want to see people saved, don't succumb to modern methods.

WHY THE DIFFERENCE?
Someone pointed out to me recently, that there was a reason the Gospel was a "stumblingblock to the Jews but foolishness to the Greeks." Why didn't it have the same effect on both? Because the Jews had the Law. Those who see the wrath of the Law abiding on them, don't see their

need of a Savior as foolishness. No, forgiveness is seen as being entirely necessary. The "stumblingblock" would seem to speak of the proud heart, *who has understanding via the Law,* but will not humble itself to believe on the name of the One they had so unjustly crucified.

AMAZING GRACE

Of all the saints who have gone before us, few would have as firm a grip on the understanding of the meaning of "grace," as the writer of Amazing Grace, John Newton. But listen to what he says of the Law - "Ignorance of the nature and design of the Law is at the bottom of most religious mistakes." In speaking of the Law's function, he said, ". . .the Law entered, that sin might abound; that the extent, the evil, and the desert of sin might be known; for it reaches the most hidden thoughts of the heart, requires absolute and perpetual obedience, and denounces a curse upon all who continue not therein." Who else in history would have an appreciation of grace like Martin Luther? Listen to what he said, "Satan. . .has raised up a sect such as teach that the Ten Commandments ought to be taken out of The Church, and that men should not be terrified by the Law, but gently exhorted by the preaching of the grace of Christ." He knew where "grace alone" preaching came from.

CONVERTING THE SOUL

If the Scriptures tell us that the Law of the Lord converts the soul (Psalm 19:7), what then is the part of the Gospel in the salvation of a sinner?

Let's look at the illustration of a man in a plane who

doesn't see his need to put a parachute on before he jumps. In fact he mocks the very thought of a parachute. How may you best convince him of his need? - by reasoning with him about the fearful consequences of breaking the law of gravity. As you, "hang him out the door by his ankles," it slowly dawns on him that if he jumps in the state he's in, he will perish. This knowledge causes him to have a complete "change of mind" about the parachute you are trying to give him. You are able to convert him to your way of thinking. When this takes place, the parachute can then do its part in saving him.

We have before us a sinner who sees no need to embrace the Gospel. He even mocks the very thought of needing to be "saved." How may you best convince him of his need? - by reasoning with him about the fearful consequences of breaking the Law of God.

As you, using the Law, hang him out the door by his ankles, it slowly dawns on him that if he died in the state he is in, he will perish under the wrath of a Holy God. This knowledge causes him to have a complete change of mind about the Gospel (the New Testament word translated "repentance," means "a change of mind"). Knowledge of the Law converts him to your way of thinking. It makes him turn completely in attitude towards the Gospel, which can save his soul. Just as knowledge of the consequences of breaking the law of gravity converted the passenger from his careless attitude to one of soberly embracing the parachute, so the perfect Law of God converts the soul, so that the sinner will gladly see his need to embrace the Savior. The Law converts the mind;

161

the Gospel saves the soul.

STICK WITH IT

If you are merely seeking decisions for Jesus, you will often be discouraged if you don't get any for a time. But if you see your task as being a *witness*, and that God is the ultimate One who saves the sinner, you will witness tirelessly "in season and out of season," trusting God to save the hearers.

Recently a young man in his early twenties knocked on the door of my friend and neighbor (and Pastor), Garry Ansdell, trying to sell encyclopedias. Garry spent about half an hour witnessing to him, bought some books, gave him some literature, and sent him on his way. The next day, the young man knocked on our door, so I witnessed to him for about 30 minutes, prayed with him that God would give him light, gave him literature, and sent him on his way. A week later, he showed up on my door step beaming from ear to ear, and said, "I got born again!" This was no "decision," attained by psychologically creeping up on the guy and having him "Shanghaied for Jesus."

When he left us, God *had* given him light. He actually read the Gospel of John *twice*, before coming to a point of repentance and faith in Jesus Christ. I am confident that this young man won't even look back to the world, because he is "fit for the Kingdom." If you read *Pilgrim's Progress* you will see that "Evangelist" was just a sign post, pointing to the light of Calvary's cross.

If you are a "true and faithful witness," you can be sure

your steps are being "ordered by the Lord." Recently one Sunday morning my steps were ordered to a store to get a washer for a faucet that wouldn't turn off. I arrived at the store at 4 minutes to 9, and was told I had to wait outside for 4 minutes. Another man was also waiting so I gave him an I.Q. Test card. I thought the guy may have been a Christian, until he cursed when he flunked the I.Q. Test. So I said "Try the other side," which is the Christian test. The small card asks a number of relevant questions about God's existence, His standards and the fact of Hell, telling the person to answer the test **"out loud."** Most actually do answer the questions out loud, letting you know their personal beliefs. This man did so, saying he didn't believe in Hell. I asked him what would happen to me if a truck was heading for me and I didn't believe in it. He saw the point. I shared that Jesus said, if you lust after a woman, you commit adultery with her in your heart, and then asked him if he had lied. He said he had. So I said (in love), "Then you're a liar." He admitted he had stolen (when he was a kid). . ."Then you're a thief. . ." As we walked into the store, he said, "And I guess I'm an adulterer. . ." Sounded like contrition so I said, "You need to repent and put your faith in Jesus Christ who died on the cross for you." Then we went our separate ways.

As we did so, within 5 seconds, the store taped music began to play John Lennon's "Imagine there's no Heaven, it's easy if you try; no Hell below us, above us only sky. . ." The timing was perfect. If God wasn't in it, I am still amazed that He would allow so many coincidences to come my way. The truth is, God promises to order our steps, if we trust and obey Him. He will bring people to you for the seed to be sown, then in His mercy lead him to other Christians for the process of reaping. (I resisted the temptation to find the guy I'd witnessed to, grab him by the shirt collar and say, "Imagine there's no truck; it's easy if you try. . .")

A friend was once telling me that before she was a Christian, while she was at a party, someone draped a pet snake around her neck. The animal slowly put a strangle hold on her to a point where Cathy became fearful for her life. She began to think that if the snake detected fear, it would squeeze her even tighter. She casually made her way outside with the snake still gripping her around the neck, and stood on the grass. Just then the owner came by and asked if the snake was putting the squeeze on her. When she said it was, he replied, "It's scared; kneel down and let it off!" She did, and the snake crawled off. . .much to her relief.

The snake-like grip of that old serpent the devil is held tightly to the throat of America. While there are those who are finding temporal pleasure in sin, others are beginning to find the truth of the words, "Whosoever serves sin is a slave of sin." Multitudes are finding themselves in bondage to alcohol, drugs, gluttony, gambling, greed, pornography etc. The only hope for this nation is for it to drop to its knees and seek God's mercy in Jesus Christ. The only way to awaken them to do so, is to preach the Law of God.

Great truth though there may be in the fact that righteousness exalts a nation, the primary object of the

Gospel is not to bring a nation into a state of prosperity, redeeming it from the bondage of sin; but its purpose is to deliver sinners from the wrath to come. Our aim shouldn't be to see revival so that we might see a "happy" America, with happy families and a smooth running economy, but it should be that we might have a nation who has fled to the Savior to find refuge from a just and holy God. Imagine if we were able to stamp out abortion, pornography, gambling etc, through legislation. All that would have happened, is that we would have gone back to the "moral" state of fifty years ago. The wrath of God would still abide on sinners.

I heard recently that Japanese authorities in Tokyo were greatly concerned about the amount of people committing suicide, by throwing themselves in front of oncoming trains at railway stations. They solved the dilemma by putting mirrors on the other side of the tracks. The suicides stopped. This happened because the last thing people want to see before they take their lives, is themselves.

So many treat the fact of their own death casually. They speak lightly of euthanasia, and of the *right* to take their own lives. Death to them is merely an end to the sufferings of this life. They need to have the mirror of the Law bought before their face. They must see themselves in truth before they die. He who has looked into the perfect Law of liberty will not be so willing to jump into death to face a Holy God, without trusting in the shed blood of the Savior.

CHAPTER 22
THE LOST ALTAR

The following information is always of interest if you have had parents: A new scientific study has revealed that, if your parents didn't have children, neither will you.

Why is the U.S. in the dilemma it is in? The reason is very clear:

"Give ear, O my people, to my law; incline your ears to the words of my mouth. I will open my mouth in a parable; I will utter dark sayings of old, Which we have heard and known, And our fathers have told us. We will not hide them from their children, Telling to the generation to come the praises of the Lord, And his strength and His wonderful works that He has done. For He established a testimony in Jacob, And appointed a law in Israel, Which He commanded our fathers, that they should make them known to their children; that the generation to come might know them, the children who would be born, and that they should arise and declare them to their children, that they may set their hope in God, and not forget the works of

God, but keep His commandments; And may not be like their fathers, A stubborn and rebellious generation, A generation that did not set its heart aright, And whose spirit was not faithful to God." Psalm 78:1-9

Notice how Israel was told to make known the Law of God to their children. Now look at Deuteronomy 6:6 (just after the Law was given to Moses) and see the same admonition: "And these words which I command you today shall be in your heart. You shall teach them diligently to your children, and shall talk of them when you sit in your house, when you walk by the way, when you lie down, and when you rise up. You shall bind them as a sign on your hand, and they shall be as frontlets between your eyes. You shall write them on the door posts of your house and on your gates." It is a sad fact that the contemporary Church has lost the family altar, particularly the teaching of God's Law to our children, and that is probably the number one reason why the Church, and thus America, is in such disarray. It has only taken a generation or two for the moral rot to set in. It wasn't too long ago that the United States could have been called a "godly" nation, esteeming the Ten Commandments. Hitler knew that the destiny of Germany would be placed into the hands of the children of the nation he ruled over; how much more should we seek to turn the tide by teaching our own children that forsaken Law.

With that thought in mind, let's take a firm grip upon eight solid rocks, and build a family altar. If you don't have any children, take these solid rocks, and pile them into the corners of your mind, so that when you do have children, they will grow up and bring delight to you, and to God.

First, let's take the solid rock of prayer. It goes without saying that we should begin devotions in a prayerful "Open my eyes, that I may see wondrous things from your Law." When the Bible speaks of the "Law," it is sometimes speaking of the entire Word of God, sometimes of the Law of Moses and sometimes of the Ten Commandments. The Ten Commandments are the very backbone of the Law of Moses and the entire Word of God. Have we ever prayed that God would open our eyes and show us wondrous things from His Law? We should only ask God to open our eyes if they are closed, so the strong implication is that the Church is either blind or asleep when it comes to the incredible things that God has in His Law. Paul, in Romans 7:22 said, "I delight in the Law of God. . ." Why do I delight in God's Law, even though I am "under grace?" - because the Law shows me God's holiness, His righteousness, His justice and truth. It is the very instrument the Holy Spirit uses to convert the soul (Psalm 19:7). It is the means by which the way to the sinner's heart is prepared to receive the grace of God. I love the Law. Yet that statement is almost anathema to the contemporary Church because it is blind to the function of the Law. I love the Law, and the devil hates it and is busy blinding the minds of them that believe not and them that believe. I know, because I was blind to salvation before I was saved, and blind to the *means* of salvation for ten years of my Christian walk. If we want to see our children truly converted, we must first know the wondrous things from His Law, and that only comes by prayer and revelation of the Holy Spirit. So the first rock is very basic; it is the solid rock of prayer.

Second, obey the command of Deuteronomy 6:6, put the Law of God in your heart, and the hearts of your children - "And these words (referring to the Law). . .shall be in your heart." Have your children memorize the Ten Commandments, and the corresponding New Testament verses. Your children will never appreciate the cross until they understand the demands of the Law. Why on earth did Jesus die? It was primarily to fulfil the demands of the Law.

Recently two boys who were fishing, tried to cross a swift stream. As they did so, a log knocked them both into deeper water. One made it to the river bank, but the other got into difficulty. A man saw him, dived in, and after a long while of fighting the current, he got the exhausted boy to the edge of the river bank. Then with both of his arms lifting the lad, he tossed him onto the bank. A woman grabbed the boy, then watched as the man sunk down into the water. She thought he was swimming to the shore. He came up once more, then drowned. Tragically, he gave his all in saving the boy, and had nothing left to save himself. Jesus said, "No greater love has a man than this, that he lay down his life for his friends."

Imagine relating that true story to someone without giving the details preceding it: "A man drowned in a river." The truth is, the danger the boy was in, the swiftness of the current, the fact that he gave his all, show what love that man had for the boy. Don't just say to your kids, "Jesus died for you on the cross;" teach them the reality of salvation, that the swift current of Eternal Justice was sweeping all humanity into the very jaws of Hell, but Jesus *gave His all* to redeem us from the "curse of the Law, being made a curse for us." Teach the Law to your children and you will help them appreciate the work of the cross.

Repetition is the mother of knowledge. What we did to help our children retain God's Word, was to repeat with them a verse six times, then give them a candy bar when they had memorized ten verses.

USE THE VISUAL MEDIUM.

I can't remember the exact statistics, but they are something like, *hear* something and you retain 10 percent; *see* something and you retain 44 percent; *see and hear* something and you retain 80 percent! So after our devotional reading, when the kids were smaller, we would have play acting. We would act out the raising of Lazarus, Daniel in the lion's den or David and Goliath. When I would throw a pillow at "Goliath," I would miss more than hit - the kids loved it and so did we. They were learning Biblical principles and having fun at the same time.

LIBERALLY USE ANECDOTES

It is said of the Messiah, "I will open my mouth in a parable" - He told stories which carried a deeper meaning; do the same. When I was on the East Coast recently, a friend pointed out a restaurant in which a doctor had eaten tuna and got food-poisoning. When the paramedics arrived he said, "Show me the E.K.G." He took one look at it and said, *"I will be dead in 15 minutes!"* He was right.

He had fifteen minutes to find peace with God - I hope he knew the way of salvation.

I heard about a woman who was in a serious car accident. As she lay dying in the hospital, she called for her mother, took her by the hand and said, "Mom, you taught me how to sew, how to cook, how to keep house. You taught me everything about living. . . *but you didn't teach me how to die!*" How do you do that? How do you teach a kid about dying?

Sue and I went to the famed Knotts Berry Farm recently with my brother-in-law who loves roller-coasters. I don't. If I want a thrill, I can go and lie down on the freeway. When he asked me to go on the insane "Montezoma's Revenge," I declined. It does a complete 360 degree loop, goes up vertically, then does the loop again *backwards!* As he walked through the gates alone, my good sense was clouded by a feeling of sorrow for him. . .and shame that Rachel, my 16 year old had been on the roller coaster five times. I gave up and went on it. The worst part was when it goes vertical and stops at the top for about two seconds. That's when your wife can see your facial expression and see if she married a man or a mouse. When I got off it, my mouse knees were weak! I was consoled by the fact that the first time Rachel went on the thing, she was terrified. The second time she was fearful, third worried, forth enjoyed it, and the fifth, bored. The more she experienced the ride, the less she was fearful. Instead of being paralysed by fear, hoping that she would get off the thing safely, she enjoyed herself, once she realized that there was nothing to fear. The roller-coaster was completely trustworthy.

That is the key to teaching your children about death. The Bible says in Romans 5:4, "experience (produces) hope." Why should we teach our children the Law and the "praises of the Lord, and His strength, and His wonderful works that He has done"? Because they can learn from the experiences of men and women of God and "set their hope in God." Those who set their hope in God are free from the power and the fear of death.

You may not realize it, but I have just used three anecdotes:

> 1/ The man who had 15 minutes to live,
> 2/ The mother who taught her daughter about everything but dying, and
> 3/ The roller-coaster experience. . .aren't anecdotes interesting? Don't they grip your attention? Follow in the steps of the greatest Teacher, open your mouth in a parable.

READ AROUND THE ROOM
Have each person in the room, audibly read a verse of Scripture. This will have a two-fold effect,

> 1/ It will build their confidence in reading out loud, and
> 2/ It will make sure they stay awake.

TALK AROUND THE WORLD
If you sat in one of our family devotions, you would probably think we were getting off the subject. You would hear us talk about T.V., how Sue and I met, the kids as

babies, school, and a million other things besides Scripture. We do this deliberately, so that we get to know our kids. If we didn't, our children are in danger of becoming passing strangers within the home.

OPEN THE SCRIPTURES TO YOUR CHILDREN

The Bible says, "The servant of the Lord must be able . . .to teach." Don't say "I can't" teach, say *"Success comes in cans"*. . ."I *can* do all things through Christ who strengthens me." Start (if you have little kids) with a "picture" Bible. I did this many years ago when I found a Bible full of beautiful pictures of Adam and Eve, Noah and the ark, David and Goliath etc. But when I turned to the New Testament, I found a picture of King Herod being presented with John the Baptist's head on a plate! His eyes were open and vacantly staring into space; so was his mouth! It was horrible. So, I got some crayons, and (God forgive me) I colored John the Baptist's head into a birthday cake. For years, my kids must have been mystified as to why King Herod's guests were so horrified by a birthday cake! An excellent book to help you if you have kids aged from 3 - 12 years is called *"Little Visits With God."* Also, have an Amplified or a Living Bible handy for difficult Scriptures.

PLOUGH THROUGH THE ICE-AGE.

Don't let anything (without being legalistic) stop you having family devotions. Your children will grow out of wanting to play David and Goliath. Around the age of thirteen, they will more than likely enter the "ice age." Instead of giggling and laughing at your jokes, or as you roll around on the floor, they will sit like blocks of ice.

Around that time you will ask yourself, *"Is it worth it all?"* Carry on regardless - it is *God's* Word, and He will watch over it. Several years ago in England a man wrote a letter to the editor of *The British Weekly*, complaining about not remembering sermons preached in church and questioning whether it was worthwhile.   He said, "I have been attending a church service. . .for the past 30 years and have heard probably 3,000 sermons. To my consternation I discovered that I cannot remember a single sermon!"

For several weeks many responded to his letter in the *Letters to the Editor* column, but the following letter finally settled the issue: "I have been married for 30 years. During that time I have eaten 32,850 meals - mostly of my wife's cooking. Suddenly, I have discovered that I cannot remember the menu of a single meal. And yet, I received nourishment from every single one of them. I have the distinct impression that without them, I would have starved to death long ago."

1 Timothy 1:5 says, "Now the purpose of the Commandment (if you read it in context, it would seem to be speaking of the Law of God) is love from a pure heart, from a good conscience, and from a sincere faith." What Sue and I are seeking to do (with the help of God) is produce love and faith, both of which will produce the other fruits of the Spirit - if you have love, you will automatically have goodness, meekness, gentleness etc., and if you have faith, that will produce peace and joy. And the third thing which we are seeking to cultivate is a good conscience, a conscience "void of offense towards God and men." The human heart is like a vault, full of contraband

goods. If I break into it, it sends out an alarm. If I don't close the door and leave, I am in danger of being taken away by the law and punished. As each of us opens the door of our heart, we find all sorts of treasures that delight our sinful souls. Jesus said, ". . .out of the heart come evil thoughts" - imaginations, lusts, unclean desires. But as we begin to take hold of the illegal goods, the conscience will send out an alarm, and if we don't heed the warning and close the door, the Law will eventually come and punish us.

As the Law is applied to the conscience of a sinner, it opens the seared conscience; but more than that, if it is continually held before the Christian, it will have the effect of keeping it soft and tender before God. If you teach your children that lust and adultery are considered the same thing in the sight of God, it will have the effect of giving them a tender conscience that will send out an alarm when there is temptation to look upon a member of the opposite sex with impure thoughts.

I often receive letters which read something like, "Johnny gave his heart to Jesus when he was four, but now that he's grown up, he's on drugs and living with his girlfriend." One thing we are not after, is a "decision" from our children. Decisions are easy to get. All you do is get a group of children into a room and say, "Kids, how do you live forever?" - "Give your heart to Jesus!" "Who wants to give their heart to Jesus?" Forest of hands - whammo fifty decisions! Trouble is, they will be fine until teenage temptation reveals their unconverted condition. All we are doing is giving ourselves and the kids a false sense of assurance. There *must* be understanding of "sin, righteousness and Judgment" before someone can be saved. Unless there is repentance, there is no salvation. Eternal life comes from "repentance towards God, and faith towards the Lord Jesus Christ."

THE PHONE BIRD

The South Island of New Zealand doesn't have crows or mocking birds; so for the first year or so in the U.S., we were fascinated by the different bird calls in California. One day, while digging a hole, I stopped to listen to the variety of songs. One in particular gripped my ears. It sounded very similar to a phone ringing. I stood there captivated by the sound. It was so close sounding to a telephone, I said to myself, "I bet Californians call it a Phone bird. Listen to it; it is almost exactly like a phone ring." Suddenly it dawned on me. It *was* the phone! I missed the caller.

Notice that when my understanding came right, the result was action. The night of my conversion, *when my understanding came right,* the result was action. When I realized I had sinned against a *holy* God, the result was repentance and faith in Jesus - "Faith comes by hearing (i.e. a right belief or understanding), and hearing, by the Word of God." I know a lady who reads her Bible out loud because she says "faith comes by hearing," but I think it means more than that. As our kids hear the Word of God, and understand God's holiness, His justice, His truth, His righteousness, His love and His faithfulness, then they will act upon the word, exercising saving faith, and come to know the salvation of God.

177

These are the eight solid rocks with which we should build the family altar: Prayer, Put the Law in the heart, Use a visual medium, Use anecdotes, Read around the room, Talk around the world, Open the Scriptures and Plough on through the "ice-age." *Now*, bind yourself to the horns of the altar in commitment to your children (if you don't have children of your own, ask God to help you find some, and teach them the Holy Scriptures), as a living sacrifice, holy and acceptable to God, "which is your reasonable service."

CHAPTER 23
TAMPERING WITH THE RECIPE

When I was a new Christian, I often quoted statistics about Christian marriages to prove the validity of the Gospel. Nowadays I don't dare. I used to point to the fact that three out of every five U.S. marriages ended in divorce, while only one in every eleven hundred ended in divorce in Christian circles. Now, I think secular and Christian divorce statistics run hand in hand. For that reason, in this chapter we will take a brief look at what makes a good Christian marriage, because, if there is one thing that will throw a child headlong into the path of sin, it's being the byproduct of a bad marriage.

WHAT IS MARRIAGE?
According to the dictionary's cold definition it's: "A legal contract entered into by a man and a woman to live together as husband and wife." Much has been said about the institution, both good and bad. A police car once stopped a motorist and informed him that his wife had fallen out of the car a mile back. "Good!" exclaimed the motorist. "I thought I'd gone deaf!" Solomon adds his experiential wisdom with, "It's better to dwell in the wilderness, than with a contentious and angry woman." In

Luke 14:20, when Jesus spoke of ones being invited to the feast, there seems to be a little dry humor present. The first man's excuse was that he had bought ground, then he gave details of why he couldn't come. The second had bought oxen, and gave details of his excuse. The third just said, "I have married a wife and cannot come." If wives seem to pick on husbands, it's often because we men deserve it. Do you know that men have to be told something *twice* before it sinks in? And have you also noticed that when God spoke to men in the Bible, in His great wisdom He often spoke twice - "Abraham, Abraham," "Samuel, Samuel," "Saul, Saul"?

Years ago, when our children were small, the moment Sue walked out the door to attend mid-week Bible study, much to the kids delight, I would jump at the recipe book to do some experimental baking. On such occasions, I would look at the instructions and be tempted to tamper with the recipe. Sometimes I would. We once made a gingerbread man and woman. I couldn't help putting in double rising powder. As we watched through the glass oven door, both the gingerbread man and woman suddenly became puffed up, then burst and merged into each other.

How often in the warmth of God's blessings we can exalt ourselves and become puffed up in pride. But if we are truly in Christ, when the intense heat of tribulation comes to us, we are suddenly bought back down to earth, and under that heat, merge as one flesh. Other cooking sprees weren't so spiritual. . .from unexpected rock cakes to peanut blackies. Sadly, because certain ingredients are missing, many Christians have either a "half-baked" marriage, which never rises to their expectations; or a marriage that crumbles in their hands. Such experiences leave a bad taste in the mouths of all concerned. So, I would like to share with you seven ingredients on how to have a good marriage.

FIRST. establish a regular prayer life together. 1 Peter 3:7 says, "Likewise, you husbands, dwell with them according to knowledge, giving honor unto the wife, as unto the weaker vessel, and as being heirs together of the grace of life; that your prayers be not hindered." Husbands and wives aren't instructed to pray together. It is taken for granted that we do. . .that we have the good sense to do everything within the confines of prayer.

If you are in a high-rise building and there's a fire, the correct thing to do is to drop to your knees; as smoke rises and you will see more clearly from that position. Make a combined marital prayer-life such second nature to you both, that the moment you find yourself in the fires of tribulation, you will drop to your knees without a second thought. You will see infinitely more on the "knees of humble faith in God," than you will from the "high hill of your own abilities" to cope with the situation.

Don't say "I don't know how to pray," say "I can do all things through Christ who strengthens me," then enter his gates with thanksgiving and His courts with praise. Thank God for a faithful partner, for a home, for life, for freedom, health, salvation etc.

SECOND. Aim to rid yourself of a selfish and sinful human nature. - "The sacrifices of God are a broken spirit and a contrite heart." What is a "broken spirit?" One who is no longer living for himself. He responds to the pull of the master's reigns. I've counseled enough marriages to know what the cause of *all* breakups is. . ."Not Thy will but mine be done!" Like the wife said to the marriage counsellor, "It all started on our wedding day. . .when *he* wanted to be in the marriage photos!" The true convert says, "I am crucified with Christ, nevertheless I live, yet not I, but Christ lives in me. . ."

THIRD. Have grace towards each other. Both parties must come to understand that "we wrestle not against flesh and blood," but against "personalities without bodies," as one modern version puts it. What is satan's will for your marriage? To kill, steal and to destroy it. So in the light of that truth we need to make certain resolutions:

A/ I will never mention divorce during an argument. Divorce is a word which should shock Christians. The more it is used as an argumentative weapon, the less distasteful it will seem. . .phrases like, "Sometimes I can really understand why some Christian marriages end in divorce!"

B/ When you are at peace, talk about what happens to your emotions during an argument. Share how you say things you don't mean. You are most vulnerable to the one you confide in most. . .we know how to hurt each other.

C/ Learn how to say "Sorry." Often I say I'm sorry, not because I think I was in the wrong, but because the argument started in the first place. You may have heard about the wife, at the end of divorce proceedings, who testified, "It all started when he walked out and slammed the door." The husband butted in, "*I didn't slam the door!*" It turned out that the wind had caught it. If only faith and humility had been there the day that happened, rather than pride and presumption.

D/ Be aware of your own faults. Remember the proverb, "Every man is pure in his own eyes." The husband who says "I have never made a mistake," has a wife who made one big one.

E/ Mutually agree never to argue in front of your children. You will lose their respect, and ruin your witness in front of those most important to you.

F/ Don't let the sun go down on your wrath. . .don't sleep on it. . .it will fester. . .and eventually poison you.

NUMBER FOUR. Feed on the Word. - "Desire the sincere milk of the word, that you might grow thereby." Psalm One promises God's blessing on all those who mediate on the Law of the Lord, "day and night." Both Sue and I have our lives ordered so that we get three meals a day. 1/ Read the word in the morning. 2/ Family devotions. 3/ Reading together each night. So many Christians are suffering from spiritual malnutrition. They are weak spiritually, and the devil is stomping all over them, something evidenced by the ship-wrecked marriages.

NUMBER FIVE. Have love and respect towards each other. Rid yourself of secular prejudice. Take for instance the Women's Liberation mentality, that the Bible looks upon the Christian husband and wife, as a "master and well-trained dog" relationship. They couldn't be further from the truth. The Bible does speak of women as the "weaker vessel," and physically this is true; but the Biblical order is, as a strong, thorny stem upholds the tender, easily-bruised, sweet-smelling rose, so should the husband uphold, love and respect his wife. Notice when you study a rose, how the leaves reach from the stem and embrace the rose. . so the arms of the husband should embrace his wife. That is God's order. Commonsense would tell me something was wrong if the stem grew out of the rose. I don't need the Bible to tell me that a cigar-smoking, tattooed, dominant woman, leading a "Yes dear" wimp called a husband, is against God's order.

The Biblical command, "Husbands, love your wives as Christ loved the Church" will only be obeyed to a point of how much you understand how much Christ loved the Church. What a place of honor and esteem our wives should have in our sight! Ladies, if your husband doesn't open the car door for you when you get home on Wednesday night after the meeting, stay in the passenger seat until he does. If however, you see the bed-room light switch off, give up and try again another time. Husbands, *if you know what's good for you,* show respect for your wife, it will become mutual, you will be rewarded. . .you will reap what you sow, and thus enrich and lift your marriage.

SIX. Communicate. The Bible says, when a man and woman are joined in marriage, "they become one flesh." Sue and I met while working in a bank. At work we were called "the budgies" because we used to sit together each day, and I would peck at her lunch. Nothing has changed. Not only is Sue my wife, she's my best friend. I don't know how itinerant preachers can stand being away from their wives for months at a time. Years ago I looked at 1 Corinthians 9:5 "Have we not power to lead about a sister, a wife, as well as other apostles, and as the brethren of the Lord, and Peter." - The Apostles took their wives with them! What God has joined, let no man separate. When I was invited to speak, I began saying, "Sorry I don't travel (internationally) without my wife". . .and God has honored it.

NEWS HOUNDS

Now here's a strange thing: in Acts 17:21 it tells us that the Athenians and strangers did nothing else but "tell or hear something new." What! Grown men sitting around like elderly ladies in a knitting circle, yapping about new things! Unbelievable! Yet they are not to be compared to modern man's insatiable appetite to hear of new things. We have news papers, Radio news, Prime-time T.V. news. Think about this sobering thought husband: If the mute button worked on your wife as well as on the T.V., and she was talking during the news, which one would you aim the remote at?

LASTLY. Expect trials. There is no avoiding it, we enter the Kingdom of God through the heat of "much tribulation." The heat will show us if we have the correct ingredients. . .it will "establish, strengthen and settle" us. So make sure you are genuine in your faith. Try always to live with a conscience "void of offense" towards both God and man, and you will never fail.

CHAPTER 24
ALL THE BETTER TO SEE YOU WITH

As the frail 5'11" 130 pound pastor walked into the living-room, a 14" blade slashed across the lower part of his neck, splattering blood on to the wall. To his horror, down came the blade a second time almost severing part of his left hand. . .a third time, this time slicing across his face. His worst nightmare had come true. . . *someone was trying to decapitate him!*

A few minutes earlier, there had been a knock at the door of the pastor's house. One of his son's had gone to the door to find a young man wanting counsel from his father. This was a little unusual as it was 3:30 am; but knowing the heart of his father, he ushered the man into the living room, while he woke the pastor. Now, just minutes later, his beloved dad was being hacked to death by a madman with a machete. He screamed for his brothers who rushed to his aid. A short time later, the man was in police custody and the pastor was in the hospital emergency room receiving masses of blood transfusions into his almost lifeless body. Miraculously, he lived. God not only restored his ministry to him, but He even healed the facial scars to a point where they are hardly noticeable.

ANOTHER CHRISTIAN?

The next day, a pastor called me and said that the incident occurred because eight years earlier, the young man had been asked to leave the church because of homosexual activity. Over those years, bitterness festered until finally it erupted in a spirit of murder.

The pastor who was speaking to me, related that the man had actually been a member of his own congregation. Still in shock, he said, "Wow. . .this is heavy. . .for another Christian to do that!" I couldn't believe what I was hearing ". . .*another Christian?*" I said, "Brother, when a member of a church tries to cut the head off the pastor, you can probably conclude that the guy lacks somewhat in love, goodness, gentleness and self control."

There's a big mystery in the modern church. It is that we are so reluctant to do what the Bible says, and "watch for wolves among the sheep." We too readily embrace everyone who names the name of Christ. The fact is, before I will let a soldier walk behind me with a fixed bayonet, I want to know that he is truly on our side, that he totally believes in our cause. I don't want him to suddenly change sides, and get a point across at my expense.

The Bible teaches that not everyone who says he is a Christian, *is* a Christian. Yet we cower at the thought of exercising biblical discernment within the Body of Christ. The Western Church has become like a fat man who swallows anything put in front of him. He hasn't the common sense to see that all that seems good, may not be beneficial to the body. This gullibility is the result of a rich, fat church, which sits at ease; a church which hasn't tasted of the chastening hand of the Lord. It is a sad fact, that it may take the machete blade of persecution to slice across the face of the church to make us take Scripture seriously.

GIFTED PREACHERS

I don't care how gifted a professing Christian is, how well he preaches, or how many miracles issue from his hands. I refuse to be impressed by leaves and branches. A fruitless professor is a Christless professor. If he abides in Christ, Jesus said he will bring forth "much fruit." Is there manifestation of love, goodness, gentleness, self control and the other fruits of the spirit? Does he have the fruit of righteousness - how does he treat his wife? How are his financial ethics? Is he humble of heart, has he a life of holiness? Is there the fruit of praise and thanksgiving? Has he the fruit of repentance? If not, you more than likely have a false convert on your hands - a stony ground hearer, of which our churches are full, from pew to pulpit.

It is my earnest hope that you are not a false convert. I trust that you have been truly "honest to God." If you haven't, that is you are harboring some secret sin, realize this, that the only one being fooled is yourself. I hope that the Law has given you a healthy fear of God, because a lack of the fear of the Lord is the cause of the problems in the contemporary church. I heard a statistic recently which seems to sum up where the Church is at. In a Gallop Poll in a survey conducted on University students among those who called themselves "evangelicals," nearly 50 percent thought it was O.K. to have premarital sex.

That shows the state of health of those professing Christians. They may think sin is O.K., but God warns that no fornicator will enter His Kingdom. Sex is a gift from God, with the clear qualification that it is only to be had within the confines of marriage. The sad fact is that these "Christians" are products of the modern soap bubble gospel. It is almost certain that they lacked repentance and "came to Jesus" for the promise of peace, love and joy.

The spiritual babe will always be awestruck with the leaves and branches of an impressive testimony, powerful preaching, fastings, even a zeal to evangelize and other (legitimate) things to make up for what a professing believer lacks in his heart. However the sunlight of persecution, temptation and tribulation will cause him to wither and die, exposing a stunted root, sitting on the shallow soil on stony ground.

Paul commanded us to "walk in wisdom toward them that are without, redeeming the time." Stony ground hearers are within the church building, but they are without the Body of Christ! They are the ones who steal time off the Pastor. They continually seek counsel, being hearers and not doers. They are satan's instrument to "wear down the saints." They are the ones who parade the dirty linen of the church before the world. At least twice in Scripture, Paul speaks of "false brethren." Take the time to go through Colossians 4:7-14 and watch Paul put a seal of approval on certain brethren, calling them "a beloved brother" saying "he is one of you," and, "receive him." Notice how he failed to put a seal on Demas. It's as though Paul wasn't convinced of the reality of his faith, so he refused to commend him as a brother in Christ. To us it may seem a little thing, but when you are living in a time of severe persecution as Paul was, the lives of the flock may be at stake. In 2 Timothy 4:10, Paul's wisdom is justified. Demas is seen to be a false conversion, "having loved this present world." If anyone "loves the world, the love of the Father is not in him" (1 John 2:15).

In Luke 10:3, Jesus did something which would be considered anathema by much of the contemporary church - He sent his lambs among wolves! Why? because He knew that the sunlight of tribulation, temptation and persecution would strengthen the genuine (those whose roots were into good soil), and expose the false. And it did. Judas, who was never a Christian, had the sunlight of temptation expose him, so that he could be seen in his true light. Jesus in reference to him said, "One of you is a devil." He would never say that of a child of God. Judas was a false convert, a thief, who deceived all but God.

In Mark 4:13 in the parable of the sower, when the disciples asked for its meaning, Jesus said, "Do you not understand this parable? How then will you understand all the parables?" In other words, the parable of the sower holds the key to unlock the mysteries of all the other parables. When we understand that the Kingdom of God has within it true and false conversions (which is what the parable of the sower is about), then the other parables begin to make sense - the wheat and tares (true and false), the foolish virgins and the wise virgins (true and false), the good fish and the bad fish (true and false), and the man who built his house on rock, and he who built it on sand.

WIDE-EYED NAIVETY

Smile if you will at the naivety of Red Riding Hood as she swallowed, wide-eyed, the lies of the wolf in Grandma's clothing. But the contemporary Church is no different. The fairy tale has a happy conclusion; you however may not have the woodman appear at your moment of need.

The next time someone professes faith in Christ, will you clap with the rest of the congregation to his response at the altar? Will you rejoice at a "decision" while Heaven reserves its rejoicing for repentance? Will you embrace him as a brother and welcome him into the flock? Will you wait until one of your youth group teenage girls becomes pregnant before you question the validity of his experience? I learned the hard way. I welcomed a guy into a local church, and I was very impressed with the leaves of an impressive testimony. The fact was, he proved to be a multiple arsonist, who threatened to murder me, stole the money from Sunday school and stole a friend's car. It could have been a lot worse.

The choice is yours. You can learn from the experience of another, or also learn the hard way. As for me and my house, we will obey the words of Jesus and "beware of false prophets, who come in sheep's clothing, but inwardly are ravening wolves." We will take heed to Paul's warning that "grievous wolves" will enter in among us, "not sparing the flock." Your choice is either to obey the Scriptures, or carry on in the spirit of naivety. If you choose to do so, go ahead, but next time you get out of bed in the middle of the night to counsel a "brother," make sure you check behind the living-room door.

CHAPTER 25
IF THE AVERAGE GIRL KNEW

A scientist once conducted an interesting series of experiments. He took two people and placed them in two studios, facing each other through a sheet of glass. Each person had a row of lights at their finger tips. As individual lights came on, they raced to switch it off. The person who turned the light off first, won. The winner then sent an electric shock into his opponent. The interesting thing was that the winner was able to choose the *degree* of shock he sent, on a one to ten scale.

The scientist found, without exception, when the players were in any way intoxicated with alcohol, the size of the shocks sent into the opponent were far greater. When the players were sober, they always sent less powerful shocks. But when they were drunk, no matter whether it was male playing female, or female playing female, or male verses male, the players became very cruel, sending maximum strength shocks if alcohol was involved. Even though the drug would seem to make a person jolly, when he is threatened in any way, most drunks become very aggressive. The conclusion was that human nature is actually very volcanic. The nicest of us has the potential to blow our tops off, if someone scratches our surface. The learned scientist could have saved himself a lot of trouble if he had taken the time to read the Bible. It says that the heart of man is "deceitfully wicked."

A concerned young Christian, in wanting to find out my opinion, showed me a letter recently. It was from a very upset person who thought that she may have homosexual tendencies.

Society has been hoodwinked into accepting many untruths, and one of the greatest is that homosexuals are "born like it." If that is true, we were all born homosexual. By that I mean that as we developed, we all had the capacity to be a homosexual. As I grew, I found that I had the potential to be a rapist, a murderer, a thief, a liar, an adulterer. In fact, as I searched deep into my own heart, I found the capacity to get into all sorts of perversions. All I discovered was a sin-full heart.

Becoming a Christian doesn't mean that you will now have a heart of purity. In fact, now more than ever you will be more conscious of your moral behavior, and sin will seem to be more evident. Whereas before you would get angry and hardly give it a second thought, now it will grieve you when sin takes rule over your will.

I have spoken with literally hundreds who are often at a point of tears because they find themselves almost burning in a battle with sexual lust. Take consolation dear Christian, you are not alone. One sign that you are a Christian, is that you *will* be battling with sin. If you are not fighting sin, it's probably because you have either surrendered to it, or maybe you have never even come across from the enemy's side. And don't think that the battle is going to become easier as you get older. I have counselled many a mature Christian (including a 74 year old man), who were battling a problem of lust. If you are a woman, dress modestly. If the average girl knew how the average guy thought, she would dress with a little more discretion. The length of some Christian girl's dresses, reveals their naivety. Girls, get this straight - there are only two sorts of men, perverts, and forgiven perverts! Show me a man (outside of Jesus Christ) who says he has never lusted, and I will show you a liar.

DIVING OR FALLING?

During the World Cup Soccer some years ago, I saw a player get foot-tripped right in front of the goal mouth. I was certain he would be awarded a penalty, but the referee waved the play on. He actually did a "Hollywood," or according to the referee, he "took a dive." The commentator agreed. If he had been tripped, he was innocent and should be compensated; but if it was deliberate, and he did take a dive, the guy was deceitful and should himself have been penalized. His *motive* was what determined his guilt or innocence. And therein lies the difference between the hypocrite and the Christian. The hypocrite *dives* into sin, while the Christian *falls*. One is innocent while the other is guilty and will receive the ultimate penalty. In the Epistle of John, there is a very comforting scripture. It says, "How do we know that we know Him? - If we keep His commandments." How do I know that I "know" the Lord? Because, for 22 years, I couldn't have cared less about God. Now, after my conversion, there is a burning desire to live to His will and honor. Nothing matters more to me than to please God. I have been given a "new heart" with new desires. Something in me *wants* to keep His Commandments, that's how I know that I know Him. When I sin, it is against my will. If I take the biggest piece of chocolate cake, suddenly I feel grieved. I don't want to be greedy, I want to be kind, caring and loving. If I sin, it's because I "fall," not because I "dive." This is the clear teaching of Scripture, "Whosoever is born of God, does not commit sin. . ." (1John 3:9). If you dive into sin, that is you get out of bed and deliberately plan to do something you know is wrong, you are in big trouble. The root of your problem is that you are more than likely a false convert - "If we say that we have fellowship with Him, and walk in darkness, we lie, and do not the truth."

Some time ago, I was speaking in the State of Texas. The Christians who had invited me to speak had warmly welcomed me into a huge nine bedroomed house. The warmth of the reception had been dwarfed a little when they told me that they caught seven scorpions in the dwelling, a week before I had arrived. Personally, I am not a great fan of scorpions, or spiders. Sue and I once walked into a bedroom in Hawaii, when Sue said, "Don't look now, *but there is a spider on the wall!*" There was. Right above my side of the bed was a huge black beast, about the size of a man's fist. It was so big, we could hear the sounds of its feet, as they walked across the wall. With careful, deliberate steps, I crept across to the other side of the room, grabbed the fly spray and sprayed the monster.

Suddenly it sprung off the wall onto our bed, and disappeared!! If we didn't locate the thing, there was no way we were going to sleep in that room. When it appeared from under the bed, I aimed the spray at the thing and fired. I think it drowned rather than died of asphyxiation.

So I wasn't exactly excited at the thought of scorpions. In fact I thought I saw one while I was speaking at the church that Sunday morning. I pointed at the carpet about 15 feet in front of me and screamed out "Scorpion!" right in the middle of the sermon. It turned out to be a large grasshopper, much to the delight of the congregation. On the Sunday evening, I was in the middle of delivering my message, when I looked down on the pulpit and saw a black spider heading towards my hand! It looked like a small tarantula so I screamed, *"Tarantula!"*, picked up a large cup of water which was on the pulpit and poured it onto the spider. The whole episode must have looked comical, because afterwards, a woman told me that she had to keep belting her husband because he was still shaking with laughter twenty minutes later.

It wasn't a tarantula as I thought. It turned out to be a "black widow," *America's most deadly spider!*

Read my words. If you are going to stand up and uncompromisingly preach God's word, there is going to be some ugly beast wanting to get his teeth into your flesh. When the Bible speaks of the "flesh," it is speaking of your sinful nature, that Adamic nature which loves to sin. When the demon of lust knocks on the door, don't answer it - tip

199

the water of the Word on its hideous head. That's what Jesus did when the devil tempted Him; He quoted the Scriptures at him, something He doesn't like at all. The effect is like shining a bright light on an ugly cockroach.

LAST WORDS

I will never forget an experience I had while ministering in Australia. During a service, an elderly man in his mid-eighties, stood up and (uninvited) rattled his way to the pulpit. The poor man was skin and bone. With trembling hands, and voice quaking with conviction, he said, "I have only one thing to say. . .and that is. . .when I was a young man. . .*I gave myself to sport*. . ." He hardly needed to say any more. Where was his physique, where was his muscle, the glory, the glitter, the splendor he attained? Listen to his wisdom. Don't waste yourself on the vanities of this life. The only difference between you and I and the elderly, is time. Now, while you are able to move, to speak, *give yourself to that which is eternal.* I'm not saying to neglect physical health; what I am saying is give some thought to your priorities. Everything you attain outside of the Kingdom of God, will eventually be torn from your hands by death. It would do every Christian a great deal of good to read a book called *Last Words of Saints and Sinners* by Herbert Lockyer. It's not the sort of book you read from cover to cover, but a few moments browsing through it tends to get the picture across. Let me quote a few last words. Firstly from Louis 17th, the King of France who died in 1795. his final words were, "*I have something to tell you*. . .!" He was either a very dry practical joker, a sadist, or one who learned the hard way, that death waits for no man.

Very memorable last words were spoken by General John Sedwick as he looked over a barricade during a battle in 1864. He boldly declared, "Stand up you cowards. . .they couldn't hit an elephant at this dist. . .!" The brilliant Albert Einstein stated some last words, but nobody knows what they were. Astute though he was, Einstein made the mistake of uttering them in his native German tongue, *which his nurse didn't understand.* Those who neglect the salvation of God reveal their foolishness by their last words. John Randolph, an American statesman of the last century cried, *"Remorse, remorse, remorse!* Let me see the word. Show me it in a dictionary. Write it then. Ah! remorse - you don't know what it means. *I cast myself on the Lord Jesus Christ for mercy!!"* Millions who reject the Gospel, sink into the horror of death in silent terror. Others who trust in Jesus, know the meaning of the last words of the famous poet John Milton, whose farewell words were, "Death is the great key that opens the palace of eternity."

It's my hope that if you and I do have any last words, they will be in the spirit of the final words of Jesus (before he died). His cry on the cross was, "It is finished!" In other words, He had completely accomplished what He set out to do. . .the will of God. Yet these weren't really His last words. After He burst from the grave, He said many things; the last recorded words were to the Apostle John, "Surely I come quickly."

Dear Christian, if you and I do die before He comes, we too will triumph over death. Our faith in Him will hold back the terrors of death. The more you cultivate faith in

God, the less fear has entry. If however, we are alive when the sky rolls back to reveal His unspeakable glory, we will be transformed from these bodies of death into incorruptible bodies, never again to experience pain, fear, loneliness, suffering, aging or death. Meditate on the marvels of the human body and this fantastic creation God has given to us. Think of the beauty of the rain forests of the Amazon, the glory of a sunset, the grandeur of the Swiss Alps, the magnificence of the Grand Canyon, and remind yourself that this is all under God's curse, that it's a fallen creation. It is nothing but a faded shadow of the "new Heavens and the new earth." The Bible tells us that our eyes have never seen, nor our ears heard, nor has it ever entered into our imaginations, the wonderful things God has in store for those that love Him.

Too many Christians are ignorant of their hope in Christ. They have little understanding of what God has for those who obey His Word. God's Kingdom is coming to this earth. . ."Thy Kingdom come, Thy will be done on earth, as it is in Heaven." This old earth is going to have the curse removed, and God's blessing dwelling upon it. When Jesus took the crown of thorns upon His head, He was taking the Genesis curse upon Himself. The starving children, the snake bites, shark attacks, scorpion bites, the pestilence, the earthquakes, cancers, floods, hurricanes, tornadoes and the seeming endless sufferings of humanity are all results of the curse. . .they are not God's perfect will.

The Bible tells us that He has "given us all things to richly enjoy," but "pleasure forevermore" is only for those who obey Him and trust in Jesus Christ.

I once read a true story, where a young man jumped from a plane for his first sky dive. When he pulled his main parachute, it failed to open. As he thought on what he was supposed to do regarding the emergency 'chute, he hit the ground. His friends rushed up to him thinking he was dead and found, miraculously, that he had landed on freshly plowed ground and was still alive. As he lay there with fourteen bones broken, and his leg bone sitting vertical from his leg, he mumbled, *"Boy did I blow it!"* He was right; he blew it. He had *listened* to his instructor; he had *believed*. . .but he hadn't *obeyed!*

Don't blow it for eternity! Listen, believe, *and* obey.

Pray that God gives you great wisdom, then pursue those who are in the shadow of death, but don't see their need to seek the mercy of God in Christ. If you don't witness of your faith, neither will you pray with passion for the lost. Your guilt will stop you praying for laborers, because you will feel like a hypocrite if you are not a laborer yourself; so the devil has a double victory because you will pray for everything but what Jesus told us to (see Matthew 9:38).

If you are fearful (and who isn't?), start your witness by using tracts. Don't even try to talk to people, just put the literature in different public places. Crawl before you walk. The time will come when God will so burden you, compassion *will* swallow your fears. I know of one man, who many years ago, received 1700 letters of salvation from people who made a commitment to Christ from a tract he had published.

Sue and I were once sitting in a doctor's waiting room. It was an ideal place to give out tracts, but as usual, I thought of 400 reasons why I shouldn't give them out on that particular occasion. First, I was with my wife and I didn't want to embarrass her by walking around the room giving out Christian literature. Second, most were reading and the last thing on their minds was God. Third, I was always giving out tracts, today I was going to have a break, etc. etc. etc. As we sat there, suddenly a three year old girl right in front of us, began to recite the Lord's prayer out loud. Then she started over again. Then again, this time louder. Everyone in the waiting room could hear her. By now, *all were thinking about God, whether they wanted to or not!* The fourth time she started, it was even louder. This time there was an air of impatience in her tone. That's when I gave in, and passed out the tracts. *Not one was refused.* God only knows, but perhaps there was a potential D.L. Moody in the room.

BE TRUE TO YOURSELF
May God give each of us the love and courage to, by any means, firmly hold passengers out the door by their ankles, until they see the seriousness of their plight. Then we will have the joy of telling them of the love of Calvary. . .giving them that glorious parachute that can save them from sure death.

If however, you have made it through this publication, and you still don't have peace with God, then your blood be upon your own head. On Judgment Day, if your eyes and my eyes meet, I will know that I am free from your blood. I have poured my heart out to you, I have reasoned with you, I have pled with you; you will have no-one to blame but yourself. If you won't be convinced of sin this side of the grave, then it will take Hell to convince you on the other side. Then you will know the full meaning of the word, "remorse." Harsh though these words may seem, God knows my motivation is one of love and concern for you.

The word atheist is made up of two Greek words, *a* - without, and *Theos* - God. *By your own choice* you are without God, and consequently, without hope.

At least be true to yourself - *drop your hypocritical "atheist" label*. You are just using the word as a very weak and transparent shield for sin. The knowledge you now have makes you more guilty than you were before you read this book. Your parachute is full of holes. You can no longer be a believer in the religion of atheism. Your faith has been shattered. You don't even believe you are an atheist. I certainly don't; neither does God. . .He calls you a *fool*. I tend to agree.

- "The fool has said in his heart, *There is no God*." Psalm 14:1

* * *

OTHER PUBLICATIONS BY RAY COMFORT:

BOOKS

Hell's Best Kept Secret (Evangelism - the forgotten key to repentance) - **$8**

The Mantle of the Harlot . . . the ultimate deception (Sequel to *Hell's Best Kept Secret*) - **$8**

Militant Evangelism (Aggressive evangelism) - **$4**

Springboards For Budding Preachers <u>Two books in one</u> (1/ Springboards - valuable "How-to's" for street preaching and personal witnessing - crammed with ear-gripping anecdotes; and 2/ *Spiritual Arson* - zeal for the lost) - **$5.50**

In Search Of New Jawbones <u>Two books in one</u> - 1/ Jawbones - zeal for the lost; and 2/ *Gospel Fire* - revival principles - **$5.50**

My Friends Are Dying! (Gripping and true story about the famed and murderous, drug infested MacArthur Park, L.A.'s area of highest crime) - **$4**

You've Got To Be Choking (Humorous illustrated look at L.A.'s air, also packed full of fascinating statistics, quality quotes and anecdotes) - **$4**

Reaching the Drug User - Drug abuse $4

God Doesn't Believe In Atheists . . . Proof The Atheist Doesn't Exist - **$7**

Russia Will Attack Israel - Excellent for unsaved - $3

TAPESETS

Words Of Comfort Six tapes - 1/ How to bring your children to Christ using the Law, 2/ Scriptures for memorization for preaching the Law, 3/ A message for America, 4/ Zeal for the lost and 2 others - **$20**

Hell's Best Kept Secret (six tapes - Why use the Law, How to use the Law and four other tapes to set you on fire for God) - **$20**

Hell's Best Kept Secret (sixteen tapes - this series contains all the tapes of the six series plus 1/ How to witness effectively, 2/ How to battle the fear of man, 3/ How to obtain zeal, 4/ The occult, 5/ Keys to revival, 6/ How to answer objections and much more) - **$48** -- *All tape messages non-copyright*

VIDEOS
Ten Cannons of God's Law (produced by Bill Gothard) - $14.95
How To Get On Fire For God - $14.95

TRACTS
COMIC TRACTS 10 cents each. **IQ CARDS $3** (Six "F"s 100). **IQ CARDS $3** (Paris In The Spring 100). **LATERAL IQ CARDS $3** (100). Natural Enquiry $4 per 100. Brain Teasers **$1.50** per 40. **Million Dollar Tracts** - $1 per pack. **Magic Johnson Tracts $5** per 100.

BOOKLETS 1/ How to Make Your Marriage Blossom, 2/ The Pit Of Hell, 3/ Freedom From Fear Of The Future, 4/ What It Means To Be A Christian - **50 cents each**
EVANGELICAL ENVELOPES - Legal size $3 (40)
T SHIRT - BREAK ONE . . . BREAK 'EM ALL - $13.95 ($1 postage)
STUDY ON THE TEN COMMANDMENTS - Twelve weeks/in vinyl folder $3.50 ($1 postage)
SLEIGHT-OF-HAND pack (Contains instructions) $17.95 ($1 postage).

CHECKS PAYABLE TO LIVING WATERS PUBLICATIONS, P.O. Box 1172 Bellflower, CA 90706 - (CA add tax)

LIVING WATERS PUBLICATIONS
P.O. Box 1172, Bellflower
CA 90706, U.S.A.
(213) 920-8431

CHECKS TO LIVING WATERS PUBLICATIONS
(please add 5 percent on books, 10 percent on tapes for
postage)

Living Waters Publications
P.O. Box 104
Blackpool, Lancs.
ENGLAND FY2 OHN

Living Waters Publications
22 Four Elms Place
Christchurch 9
NEW ZEALAND

Living Waters Publications
P.O. Box 240
Hatteras
NC 27943, U.S.A.

Living Waters Publications
Box 446 Stn A
Kelowna B.C.
CANADA

Living Waters Publications
P.O. Box 202
Vermont, Vict 3133
AUSTRALIA